THE
UNPROCESSED
AIR FRYER

JENNY TSCHIESCHE

hamlyn

To all those out there living busy
lives who simply want to eat
delicious food, cooked quickly from
scratch, may this book inspire you.

hamlyn

First published in Great Britain in
2025 by Hamlyn, an imprint of
Octopus Publishing Group Ltd
Carmelite House
50 Victoria Embankment
London EC4Y 0DZ
www.octopusbooks.co.uk

An Hachette UK Company
www.hachette.co.uk

The authorized representative in
the EEA is Hachette Ireland,
8 Castlecourt Centre,
Dublin 15, D15 XTP3, Ireland
email: info@hbgi.ie

Text copyright
© Jenny Tschiesche 2025

Photography, design and layout
copyright © Octopus Publishing
Group Ltd 2025

Distributed in the US by
Hachette Book Group
1290 Avenue of the Americas,
4th and 5th Floors,
New York, NY 10104

Distributed in Canada by
Canadian Manda Group
664 Annette St., Toronto, Ontario,
Canada M6S 2C8

ISBN 978 0 60063 906 0
eISBN 978 0 60063 907 7

A CIP catalogue record for
this book is available from the
British Library.

Printed and bound in China.
10 9 8 7 6 5 4 3 2

Publisher: Kate Fox
Senior Managing Editor:
 Sybella Stephens
Copy Editor: Jo Smith
Art Director: Juliette Norsworthy
Designer: Nicky Collings
Photographer: Clare Winfield
Food Stylist: Laura Field
Props Stylist: Zoe Harrington
Production Controllers: Lucy Carter
 & Nic Jones

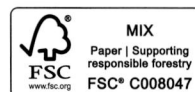

FSC
www.fsc.org

MIX
Paper | Supporting
responsible forestry
FSC® C008047

CONTENTS

INTRODUCTION

In today's fast-paced world, convenience often takes precedence over nutrition. Ultra-processed foods (UPFs), with their long shelf lives and enticing flavours, have become a staple in many households. It's hard to avoid these foods as they're all over our supermarkets. They come with promises of being 'deliciously irresistible', of having a 'great new flavour', or being 'low fat' or 'lower in sugar'. In our increasingly fast-paced lives, the promise of something that seems like a healthier option, that tastes great and is almost ready to go from the packet, is a compelling one. However, as a nutritionist, I have witnessed firsthand the detrimental effects these foods can have on our health. This book sheds light on the science behind ultra-processed foods and provides practical strategies for reducing their consumption.

WHAT ARE UPFs?

There has been a surge of interest in ultra-processed foods in recent years, but what actually are they? Ultra-processed foods are, put simply, foods that you couldn't make in an ordinary home kitchen. Processing involves deconstructing normal foods and reconstructing them again using chemical processes. Typically, UPFs contain ingredients that sound like they belong in a science lab, not a home kitchen, such as artificial flavourings, emulsifiers, colouring, stabilizers, acidity regulators, sweeteners and preservatives.

Although many people assume that the worst offenders will be fast food and junk food, there are some surprises when it comes to foods that contain ultra-processed ingredients. As our shopping habits have become increasingly centralized, manufacturers have to concentrate on finding ways to increase shelf life, replace flavours lost during the manufacturing process and create familiar textures in unfamiliar foods. UPFs are vital for these processes, but mean that you find them in very common products, including shop-bought bread, most breakfast cereals, many snack foods (even those marketed as healthy), fruit-flavoured yogurts, many shop-bought soups, most shop-bought sandwiches and nearly all sauces.

In fact, so-called ultra-processed foods count for 56 per cent of calories consumed by adults across the UK, and 65 per cent of those consumed by children.[1] In the US, the figure is closer to 60 per cent in adults and 70 per cent in children.[2]

These foods are cheaper and have a much longer shelf life, but sadly this ultra processing has negative consequences for our health.

1 Global Food Research Program, 'Ultra-processed foods: A global threat to public health', May 2021.
2 Statista, 'The health effects of ultra-processed food - Statistics & Facts', September 2024.

WHY SHOULD WE CARE?

Ultra-processed foods are more than just a dietary choice; they are a significant factor in the rising rates of obesity, diabetes, heart disease and even mental health disorders. These foods are engineered to be hyper-palatable, making them difficult to resist and easy to overconsume. They are often stripped of essential nutrients and contain unhealthy fats, sugars and additives which can wreak havoc on our bodies.

Several studies looking at large numbers of people have shown that those who eat a diet that is high in UPFs have higher rates of cardiovascular disease (which includes diseases such as heart attacks and strokes), diabetes, obesity and kidney disease.

At a recent meeting of the American Society for Nutrition in Chicago, an observational study of more than 500,000 people in the US was revealed, which showed that those who ate the most ultra-processed foods had a roughly 10 per cent greater chance of dying early, even accounting for their body mass index and overall quality of diet.

In recent years, lots of other observational studies have shown a similar link. A link is not the same as proving that food processing is detrimental to our health, but it is becoming clear that UPFs play a part in contributing to long-term health problems.

ULTRA-PROCESSED FOODS ARE DIFFICULT TO RESIST AND EASY TO OVERCONSUME

There are now several animal-based studies that show that ultra-processed ingredients promote systemic inflammation through the interaction of components with the gut microbiome. This change in microbes in the gut may be due to a lack of fibre and nutrient-rich components found in unprocessed food. The effects of inflammation in the body have been widely studied. Inflammation is associated with increased risk of developing gut disease like Crohn's, IBS and colitis, cardiovascular disease including stroke and heart attack, and even mental health problems too.

It is also a fact that manufacturers use processing to make food hyper-palatable – the more delicious it is, the more consumers will buy it. But it also means people eat more of it. UPFs can be highly addictive and override the body's normal ability to stop eating once full. This is one of the key reasons why UPFs are contributing to the obesity crisis in many countries worldwide.

WHAT CAN I DO ABOUT IT?

When we are confronted with facts and statistics like this, it can feel alarming and overwhelming. Even if you want to avoid UPFs, you still need the way you eat to fit in with your everyday life.

As a nutritionist, I am interested in how our health is influenced not only by the nutrient content of the food we eat, but also through the processes used to make it and preserve it.

Being a busy working mother, I want quick and healthy solutions. To be honest, I would go so far as to call myself 'the cheat's cook'. I simply want an easy way to get tasty yet unprocessed food on the table.

You don't need to be a nutritionist to eat this way though. It really is as simple as reading ingredients labels. If the ingredients list on the label of a food product features strange and chemical-sounding names, then the chances are it falls into the ultra-processed category.

It's important that we don't demonize any one type of food. That's simply not helpful, especially when what and how to eat is such a complicated issue. So instead, rather than trying to eliminate all ultra-processed foods, it's better to just reduce the amount you're eating.

SURPRISING FOODS YOU SHOULD CHECK THE LABEL ON

KETCHUP, MAYONNAISE
& MUSTARD

SOY SAUCE

GREEK YOGURT

BREAD & WRAPS

CEREAL BARS

SOUPS

SOURDOUGH

SALAD DRESSINGS

WHY USE AN AIR FRYER?

I am a huge fan of the air fryer, which can simply be thought of as a smaller, faster, more powerful oven. Having access to an air fryer makes it so much easier to cook quickly, removing the barrier of time from scratch cooking. An air fryer doesn't take up too much space in the kitchen and they are so easy to use that even my teenagers willingly cook meals from scratch themselves.

HOW TO USE AN AIR FRYER

There are now several different types of air fryer on the market, from those with large drawers to those with small drawers, and even some with multiple drawers, either side by side or stacked. Some don't have any drawers at all, appearing more like a traditional oven, with several shelves to cook on. The recipes in this book are designed for a medium-sized air fryer so you may need to cook in batches in a smaller model, or scale down the recipe accordingly. If you have a larger air fryer, you can also scale up the recipes to feed more people.

When choosing an air fryer, you really only need a model that air fries. Some have other functions, such as grill and dehydrate settings, but the recipes in this book are designed for air frying only. Many offer baking and roasting buttons too, but usually these are simply programmes set by the manufacturer to best emulate baking and roasting. Once you get the air fryer home, you can change these presets to suit your own cooking, but as the function is still air frying, I would simply use the air fry button and adjust the time and cooking temperature accordingly.

Having used air fryers regularly for well over five years, I have certainly discovered how to get the most out of these wonderful appliances. Here are some of my top tips:

- Use a meat thermometer – this is highly recommended for safety reasons because with air frying, looks can be deceiving thanks to the speed food cooks, but it will also give you confidence over time to know how long to cook food.

- Many recipes need to be cooked in a baking dish, tin, tray or ramekin inside the air fryer. What you choose to cook in may affect the speed of cooking as some materials will take longer to heat up.

- Don't use metal implements inside your air fryer because they can damage the lining.

- Ovenproof mittens rather than ovenproof gloves are recommended for removing hot dishes from the air fryer, simply because they're less cumbersome.

- Silicone tongs are helpful for turning and removing food during and at the end of cooking, without damaging your air fryer.

THE UNPROCESSED PANTRY

There are so many sauces and dressings we rely on for everyday cooking, but shop-bought versions can often be ultra processed. The following basic recipes on pages 10–11 show how simple it is to make them from scratch, offering a huge reward for very little effort. I make batches of vegetable stock and tomato sauce and always keep a few portions in the freezer. Having some on hand means you're less likely to fall back on convenient UPF alternatives.

As well as the following basic recipes, there are other delicious UPF-free recipes in the book that can be used to accompany a range of different dishes, including Tzatziki on page 57, Guacamole on page 46, Pickled Cucumber on page 116, Tomato Salsa on page 112 and Mango & Avocado Salsa on page 129.

VEGETABLE STOCK PASTE

MAKES 550ML
(ABOUT 1 PINT)

Making your own might seem like a hassle but it is one of the many UPF-free wins in terms of cost – stock paste is so much cheaper to make than it is to buy.

1 tablespoon extra virgin olive oil

6 small garlic cloves, peeled

2 courgettes, cut into large chunks

2 tomatoes, quartered

2 red onions, roughly chopped

2 carrots, finely chopped

3 celery sticks, roughly chopped

150g (5½oz) coarse sea salt

3 tablespoons chopped parsley with stems

2 tablespoons chopped basil with stems

Heat the olive oil in a wide saucepan over a medium-high heat and add the garlic, all the vegetables and the salt. The vegetables will start to release their liquid. Keep stirring until the liquid almost covers the vegetables, then leave it to simmer rapidly for about 30 minutes, until more than half the liquid has evaporated.

Add the herbs and leave to cook for 2 more minutes, then allow to cool.

Blend the mixture in a blender or food processor until smooth, then transfer to sterilized jars. Store in the fridge for up to 3 months, or the freezer for up to a year.

UBIQUITOUS TOMATO SAUCE

MAKES 4 JARS,
ABOUT 330ML
(11FL OZ) EACH

A simple pasta sauce, and an ingredient used in several recipes in this book, including Chicken Parmesan (see page 49), Beef Meatballs (see page 59) and Gnocchi Bake (see page 75). This sauce has the consistency of ready-made tomato pasta sauce found in jars.

1 tablespoon extra virgin olive oil

500g (1lb 2oz) chopped mixed carrot, onion and celery (fresh or frozen)

1 tablespoon chopped garlic

2 teaspoons Vegetable Stock Paste (see above)

1 tablespoon tomato purée

2 teaspoons unrefined sugar

2 x 400g (14oz) cans UPF-free plum tomatoes

1 teaspoon dried oregano

1 teaspoon dried basil

salt and pepper

Heat the olive oil in a saucepan over a medium heat. Add the vegetables and garlic and cook until softened; this should take 5–10 minutes. Add the stock paste, tomato purée, sugar, plum tomatoes and herbs. Use a potato masher to break down the tomatoes, bring to the boil, then simmer for 10 minutes. If it becomes too thick, add a little water. Taste and season if necessary. Leave to cool, then blitz in a food processor until smooth. Store in clean jars in the fridge for up to 5 days, or airtight containers in the freezer for up to 3 months.

TARTARE SAUCE

If you pick up a jar of tartare sauce in the supermarket, you'll commonly find it contains sweeteners, sugar, starches, stabilizers and preservatives. This homemade version uses well-recognized kitchen ingredients. It is based on a BBC Good Food recipe I have been using for some time.

5 cornichons, drained

1 tablespoon capers, drained

1½ teaspoons lemon juice

1 tablespoon chopped parsley

1 tablespoon chopped tarragon

6 tablespoons UPF-free mayonnaise

Blitz all the ingredients, except the mayonnaise, in a mini food processor to combine. Fold the ingredients into the mayonnaise until well mixed. Alternatively, finely chop all the ingredients by hand, then mix with the mayonnaise in a bowl. Refrigerate until ready to serve.

GARLIC BUTTER

MAKES 70G (2½OZ)

60g (2¼oz) salted butter, softened

1 teaspoon crushed garlic

Mix the butter and garlic together thoroughly in a bowl.

VINAIGRETTE DRESSING

MAKES 5 TABLESPOONS

This simple dressing can be used for a variety of different salads, from the Roasted Spiced Carrot Salad on page 33 and the Sweet Potato, Blue Cheese & Walnut Salad on page 106, to a simple green salad.

½ shallot, finely chopped

1 tablespoon white wine vinegar

1 tablespoon lemon juice

1 tablespoon extra virgin olive oil

1 tablespoon maple syrup

Place all the ingredients in a screw-top jar and shake to combine. Store any leftovers in the fridge for up to a week.

WHERE TO BEGIN

Since there are more than 100 recipes in this book, some suited to every eventuality, I'd encourage you to experiment with them until you find your favourites. Here are a few of mine.

FOR DRINKS WITH FRIENDS

Parma Ham Chips (see page 166)

Chilli & Lime Chickpeas (see page 164)

Padrón Peppers (see page 163)

Spiced Cashews (see page 167)

FOR FAMILY DINNERS

Lamb Kofta Burgers with Tzatziki
  (see page 57)

Chicken Parmesan (see page 49)

Chicken Fajitas (see page 46)

Chicken Stir-Fry (see page 70)
  with brown rice or noodles

Beef Meatballs (see page 59)

FOR QUICK AFTER-WORK SUPPERS

Honey-Glazed Salmon (see page 43)
  with brown rice and Pickled
  Cucumber (see page 116)

Creamy Mushroom Pasta Sauce
  (see page 53) with fresh pasta

Gnocchi Bake (see page 75)

Taco-Stuffed Sweet Potatoes
  (see page 85)

Chorizo & Pork Burgers
  (see page 65)

FOR HEALTHY BREAKFASTS & BRUNCHES

Granola (see page 155)
  with Greek yogurt

Soft-Boiled Eggs & Soldiers
  (see page 34)

Creamy Mushrooms on Toast
  (see page 88)

Egg, Spinach & Parma Ham Pots
  (see page 22)

Cashew Butter (see page 167)
  on sourdough toast

Roasted Figs with Goats' Cheese
  (see page 29)

SHOWSTOPPERS

Miso Salmon with Broccoli (see page 109)

Halloumi, Honey & Parma Ham
  Salad (see page 25)

Baked Butternut Squash (see page 92)

Fish Tacos with Mango & Avocado Salsa
  (see page 129)

Halloumi Baked Mushrooms
  (see page 51)

Cod Wrapped in Parma Ham
  (see page 102)

COMPLETE AIR FRYER MEALS

Menu 1: Vegetarian

Bruschetta (see page 101)

Halloumi & Courgette Kebabs
(see page 54)

Mediterranean Veg & Couscous Salad
(see page 142)

Baked Cinnamon Nectarines
(see page 174)

Menu 2: End of the Week

Roasted Red Pepper & Tomato Soup
(see page 30)

Taco-Stuffed Sweet Potatoes
(see page 85)

Corn on the Cob (see page 135)

Fruit Crumble Pots (see page 182)

Menu 3: Impressing Friends

Roasted Spiced Carrot Salad
(see page 33)

Chicken Tikka (see page 115)

Tandoori Cauliflower (see page 147)

Baked Strawberry 'Cheesecakes'
(see page 170)

Menu 4: An Unprocessed Picnic

UPF-Free Scotch Eggs (see page 80)

Stuffed Tomatoes (see page 50)

Hard-Boiled Egg Sandwiches
(see page 39)

Moroccan-Style Carrot Hummus
(see page 159)

Aubergine & Yogurt Dip
(see page 160)

Roasted Pepper & Walnut Dip
(see page 159)

Garlic Pitta Chips (see page 163)

Apple Chips (see page 152)

Simple Banana Bread (see page 186)

QUICK & EASY
LUNCHES

BACON & ROAST TOMATO BAPS

When looking to reduce processed foods, bottled sauces are a great place to start and here we replace ketchup with succulent tomatoes. Roasting tomatoes with some seasoning and a little honey brings out their natural sweetness, which contrasts so well with the salty bacon in this delicious bap. Avoid bacon that contains nitrates.

SERVES 2

1 tomato, finely chopped

⅛ teaspoon salt

⅛ teaspoon pepper

⅛ teaspoon runny honey

⅛ teaspoon extra virgin olive oil

4 back bacon rashers

1 tablespoon butter

2 UPF-free baps, cut in half

Preheat the air fryer to 180°C (350°F).

Mix the tomato with the salt, pepper, honey and olive oil. Divide between 2 ramekins and cook in the air fryer for 6–8 minutes, stirring half way. If you have sufficient room in your air fryer, cook the bacon with the tomato for 6 minutes, turning half way through. If there's not enough room, cook the bacon separately.

Meanwhile, butter the baps. Once both the bacon and tomato are cooked, serve inside the baps.

BAKED EGGS WITH CHORIZO, SPINACH & TOMATO

This is an ideal lunch or brunch recipe. Look for nitrate-free chorizo (the way it is traditionally made). You may need to halve this recipe if you have a smaller air fryer.

SERVES 2

160g (5¾oz) frozen spinach, defrosted

60g (2¼oz) nitrate-free chorizo, chopped

300g (10½oz) passata

½ teaspoon salt

¼ teaspoon pepper

1 teaspoon balsamic vinegar

4 eggs

bread, to serve (optional)

Preheat the air fryer to 180°C (350°F).

Squeeze as much water as you can from the spinach. Place it in a bowl with the chorizo, passata, salt, pepper and vinegar, stir together, then pour into a heatproof dish that fits in the air fryer.

Make 4 wells in the mixture and crack in the eggs. Cook in the air fryer for 13–15 minutes, or until the eggs are just cooked. Serve with bread, if liked.

COURGETTE-CRUST MINI QUICHES

Courgette provides an ideal 'crust' for these mini quiches, which are packed full of flavour. Use a vegetable peeler to slice the courgette very thinly.

SERVES 2

1 teaspoon extra virgin olive oil

1 courgette, very thinly sliced lengthways

4 large eggs, beaten

120g (4¼oz) sun-dried tomatoes, chopped

120g (4¼oz) Parmesan cheese, very finely grated

salad leaves, to serve (optional)

Preheat the air fryer to 200°C (400°F).

Brush 4 ramekins with the olive oil, then line them with the slices of courgette to form the bases and sides of the quiches.

Place the eggs in a bowl and stir in the sun-dried tomatoes and cheese. Pour the mixture into the ramekins and cook in the air fryer for 13–15 minutes, or until the egg is set and the courgette has contracted away from the sides of the ramekins.

Leave to cool a little before removing from the ramekins and serve with salad leaves, if you like.

EGG, SPINACH & PARMA HAM POTS

Parma ham is one of the few hams that can be easily found without added preservatives. Here, thinly sliced Parma ham makes an ideal 'crust' for these delicious egg pots, which make a quick and easy lunch.

SERVES 2

8 slices of Parma ham

40g (1½oz) Red Leicester cheese, grated

2 tomatoes, chopped

40g (1½oz) spinach leaves, chopped

4 eggs, beaten

salad leaves, to serve (optional)

Preheat the air fryer to 200°C (400°F).

Line 4 ramekins with 2 slices of Parma ham each, covering the bases and sides.

Mix all the other ingredients in a bowl and divide between the ramekins, pushing the spinach down below the level of the egg where possible (it doesn't matter if a little sticks out).

Cook in the air fryer for 15 minutes, or until the egg is set. Carefully prise the crust away from the edges of the ramekins with a knife. Remove from the ramekins and serve with salad leaves, if you like.

HALLOUMI, HONEY & PARMA HAM SALAD

Look for Parma ham with just two ingredients – pork and salt – but no other preservatives. I recommend preparing this when peaches and nectarines are fully ripe, for the best flavour combination.

SERVES 2
*AS A LUNCH OR
4 AS A STARTER*

4 slices of Parma ham, halved

250g (9oz) halloumi, cut into 8 fingers

1½ teaspoons runny honey

30g (1oz) rocket

2 ripe white or yellow peaches or nectarines, pitted and cut into wedges

2 teaspoons olive oil

1 teaspoon balsamic vinegar

pepper

Preheat the air fryer to 180°C (350°F).

Lay the slices of Parma ham on a board and place a halloumi finger on each. Drizzle over half the honey, then wrap the cheese in the ham. Add to the air fryer in a single layer and cook for 8–10 minutes.

Meanwhile, prepare the salad – toss the rocket and peaches in the olive oil and balsamic vinegar with a good pinch of pepper.

Serve the salad with the hot ham-wrapped halloumi on top, drizzled with the remaining honey.

MINI FLATBREAD QUICHES

Flatbreads often contain far fewer and more recognizable ingredients than tortilla wraps, so these quiches use mini flatbreads as their crust. They're ideal for a quick lunch. Use fresh pesto, or one from a jar, but seek out a brand with minimal additives.

MAKES 2

½ teaspoon olive oil

2 mini UPF-free flatbreads

1 large egg

2 teaspoons UPF-free pesto

15g (½oz) Parmesan cheese, finely grated

pepper

rocket salad, to serve (optional)

Preheat the air fryer to 180°C (350°F).

Brush 2 ramekins with the olive oil, then pop a flatbread in each.

Beat the egg and stir in the pesto, cheese and a good pinch of pepper. Divide the mixture evenly between the ramekins.

Cook in the air fryer for 10–12 minutes, or until the egg is set. Allow to cool a little before turning the mini quiches from the ramekins. Serve with a rocket salad, if you like.

ROASTED FIGS WITH GOATS' CHEESE

What a wonderful pairing – sweet and spicy roasted figs with tangy goats' cheese! Great for a quick and easy lunch for two.

6 ripe figs, stems trimmed

1 teaspoon ground cinnamon

2 teaspoons runny honey

1 teaspoon water

200g (7oz) soft goats' cheese

4 slices of sourdough toast, to serve

Preheat the air fryer to 180°C (350°F).

Place the figs in a heatproof dish that fits in the air fryer. Sprinkle over the cinnamon, drizzle over the honey and then the water and give everything a stir. Cook in the air fryer for 15–20 minutes, or until the figs squash with the back of a fork and have a jammy feel and look.

Spread the goats' cheese on to the toast with the back of a spoon and serve the roasted figs on top.

ROASTED RED PEPPER & TOMATO SOUP

SERVES 4

Roasting vegetables in an air fryer really brings out their flavour. As stock cubes often contain UPFs, I recommend making your own stock paste (see page 10).

3 tomatoes, quartered

2 red peppers, cored, deseeded and cut into wedges

1 red onion, cut into 8 wedges

2 small garlic cloves, peeled

1 tablespoon extra virgin olive oil, plus extra to serve

½ teaspoon salt

½ teaspoon dried oregano

300ml (½ pint) hot water

½ teaspoon Vegetable Stock Paste (see page 10)

1 teaspoon runny honey

5 tablespoons double cream, plus extra to serve

Preheat the air fryer to 200°C (400°F).

Place the tomatoes, peppers, onion and garlic in a heatproof dish that fits in the air fryer, add the olive oil, salt and oregano and toss (you may need to do this in 2 batches). Cook in the air fryer for 20 minutes, giving the vegetables an occasional stir, until soft.

Blitz the cooked vegetables in a food processor with the hot water, stock paste, honey and cream.

Reheat the soup in the heatproof dish in the air fryer for a few minutes before serving with an extra swirl of cream.

ROASTED CURRIED VEG SOUP

SERVES 2

This is a great prepare-ahead lunch to take to work or school. It is also great for using up leftover vegetables. Its velvety texture and rich flavour make this an ideal winter warmer. Choose a curry powder without added starches, flours or fillers.

200g (7oz) cauliflower florets

200g (7oz) carrots, cut into batons the same size as the cauliflower

1 tablespoon extra virgin olive oil, plus extra to serve

1 teaspoon UPF-free medium curry powder

½ teaspoon unrefined sugar

¼ teaspoon salt

400ml (14fl oz) hot water

1 teaspoon Vegetable Stock Paste (see page 00)

160ml (5½fl oz) UPF-free coconut cream

Preheat the air fryer to 180°C (350°F).

Toss the vegetables in a bowl with the olive oil, curry powder, sugar and salt. Transfer to a heatproof dish that fits in the air fryer, then cook for 20 minutes, or until they're soft.

Remove carefully from the air fryer and blitz the vegetables in a food processor with the hot water, stock paste and coconut cream.

Reheat the soup in the heatproof dish in the air fryer for a few minutes before serving with an extra drizzle of olive oil.

ROASTED SPICED CARROT SALAD

Air fryers and salads don't immediately seem to go together, until you think of an air fryer as a compact oven and roasted vegetables as a delicious salad component. These sweet and spicy roast carrots are served with peppery rocket, creamy soft goats' cheese and earthy walnuts, all brought together by a delicious vinaigrette dressing.

SERVES 2

250g (9oz) carrots, cut into 8mm (⅜ inch) thick diagonal slices

½ teaspoon ground cumin

½ teaspoon ground coriander

¼ teaspoon sumac (optional)

¼ teaspoon salt

⅛ teaspoon pepper

1 tablespoon extra virgin olive oil

70g (2½oz) rocket leaves

100g (3½oz) soft goats' cheese, in small pieces

40g (1½oz) walnuts, roughly chopped

2 tablespoons Vinaigrette Dressing (see page 11)

Preheat the air fryer to 180°C (350°F).

Toss the carrots in a bowl with the spices, salt, pepper and olive oil. Place in a heatproof dish that fits in the air fryer and cook for 20 minutes, stirring twice during cooking. Leave to cool a little.

Place the rocket, goats' cheese and walnuts in a salad bowl, toss in the roast carrots and stir everything together with the dressing.

SOFT-BOILED EGGS & SOLDIERS

This is a fuss-free way to prepare soft boiled eggs. Make sure your eggs are at room temperature before you begin – take your eggs out of the fridge at least 30 minutes before you want to cook them – otherwise you may end up with unevenly cooked eggs.

SERVES 2

4 eggs, at room temperature

2 slices of rustic bread

2 tablespoons salted butter

Preheat the air fryer to 180°C (350°F).

Place the eggs in the air fryer and cook for 6 minutes. If there's room for the bread too, add that at the same time and turn half way through cooking. If not, toast the bread in a toaster.

Butter the toast and slice it into soldiers for dipping. Quickly slice the tops off the eggs and enjoy. Don't leave the eggs for too long before you slice off the tops as they will carry on cooking in the shells.

TUNA & WHITE BEAN SWEET POTATO

Here the classic Mediterranean salad combination of tuna and white beans is given a twist. Served in baked sweet potatoes, the acidity of the tuna and bean salad perfectly marries the starchy sweetness of the potato.

SERVES 2

2 sweet potatoes

145g (5¼oz) can tuna in oil, drained

150g (5½oz) canned butter beans or cannellini beans, drained

½ red onion, finely diced

2 tablespoons UPF-free mayonnaise

juice of 1 small lime

½ red chilli, deseeded and finely chopped

salt and pepper

finely diced cucumber, to garnish

rocket leaves, to serve (optional)

Preheat the air fryer to 180°C (350°F).

Prick the sweet potato skins, place them in the air fryer and cook for 30–35 minutes, or until they just give when a fork is inserted.

Meanwhile, in a bowl, mix together all the remaining ingredients, except the cucumber.

Once the potatoes are cooked, leave to cool a little, then slice open and fill with the tuna mixture. Top with finely diced cucumber and serve with some rocket leaves, if you like.

CREAMY COURGETTE SOUP

The air fryer is a great tool for roasting vegetables for soups. The vegetables cook quickly and caramelize easily, which means soups made this way are packed full of flavour.

1 courgette, cut into 1cm (½ inch) thick slices

1 red onion, cut into 8 wedges

1 tablespoon extra virgin olive oil

2 garlic cloves

270ml (9½fl oz) hot water

½ teaspoon Vegetable Stock Paste (see page 10)

2 tablespoons double cream

15g (½oz) Parmesan cheese, finely grated

¼–½ teaspoon pepper

salt

Preheat the air fryer to 180°C (350°F).

Toss the vegetables in a bowl with the olive oil, a pinch of salt and the unpeeled garlic cloves. Transfer to a heatproof dish that fits in the air fryer, then cook for 20 minutes, or until they're soft, tossing the vegetables occasionally. You may need to do this in 2 batches, depending on the size of your air fryer.

Allow to cool a little, then squeeze out the garlic flesh and discard the skins. Blitz the vegetables and garlic in a food processor with the hot water, stock paste, cream, cheese and pepper.

If you need to reheat the soup before serving, pop it back into the heatproof dish in the air fryer for a few minutes, or transfer to a saucepan.

HARD-BOILED EGG SANDWICHES

This is possibly the easiest way to prepare both soft-boiled and hard-boiled eggs, allowing you to quickly and easily make this classic sandwich filling. While egg and cress is the usual combination, egg and watercress is much more nutritious and has a wonderful peppery flavour.

SERVES 2–3

6 eggs, at room temperature

4 tablespoons UPF-free mayonnaise

30g (1oz) cress or watercress, roughly chopped

salt and pepper

4–6 slices of bread, to serve

Preheat the air fryer to 180°C (350°F).

Cook the eggs in the air fryer for 10 minutes. Once cooked, carefully remove the eggs from the air fryer using an oven mitt and place in a bowl of ice-cold water to cool.

Peel the eggs, then chop them and mix with the mayonnaise, cress or watercress and salt and pepper to taste. Use the egg filling to make sandwiches with the bread.

MIDWEEK
MEALS

HONEY-GLAZED SALMON

If you compare effort with outcome, this dish is a winner. For very little effort, you have a lip-smacking dish in under 15 minutes. This combination of honey, soy sauce and chilli oil really does give any shop-bought Asian marinade a run for its money.

SERVES 2

1 tablespoon chilli oil

1 teaspoon soy sauce

1 teaspoon runny honey

400g (14oz) skinless salmon fillet, cut into 2cm (¾ inch) cubes

300g (10½oz) asparagus spears

½ teaspoon olive oil

salt and pepper

lime wedges, to serve

Preheat the air fryer to 180°C (350°F).

Place the chilli oil, soy sauce and honey in a heatproof dish that fits in the air fryer, mix well, then add the salmon cubes and toss to coat. Arrange the salmon in a single layer. If you have a smaller air fryer, you may need to cook in batches.

Toss the asparagus in the olive oil with some salt and pepper. Place the salmon dish in the air fryer with the asparagus alongside and cook for 12 minutes, or until the salmon is cooked through (if you have a meat thermometer, the internal temperature should be 63°C/145°F). Serve with lime wedges for squeezing over.

CAJUN CHICKEN SKEWERS

While it is tempting to reach for packet mixes of chicken marinade, they can contain added ingredients such as starches and sweeteners. The combination of spices in this recipe is easy to create from your kitchen spice store. With a short marinating time, these chicken skewers are deliciously spiced, wonderfully moist and super-quick to make.

SERVES 4

3 tablespoons extra virgin olive oil

2 tablespoons lime juice

2 teaspoons ground cumin

2 teaspoons ground coriander

2 teaspoons smoked paprika

1 teaspoon dried oregano

¾ teaspoon salt

¼ teaspoon pepper

700g (1lb 9oz) chicken breast mini fillets

TO SERVE (OPTIONAL)

lemon wedges

UPF-free flatbreads

Greek yogurt

fresh coriander leaves

Mix the olive oil, lime juice, spices, oregano and salt and pepper in a large bowl, add the chicken breast fillets, toss to coat, cover, then leave to marinate in the fridge for 1 hour.

Preheat the air fryer to 180°C (350°F).

Thread the fillets lengthways on to metal or soaked wooden skewers, then cook in the air fryer for 12 minutes, turning once, or until cooked through (if you have a meat thermometer, the internal temperature should be 74°C/165°F).

Serve the chicken on or off the skewers with lemon wedges. I like to serve it in flatbreads with Greek yogurt and corinder leaves.

CHICKEN FAJITAS

You may be surprised by the added ingredients in shop-bought fajita spice mixes. I use this homemade version to make delicious and moist chicken fajitas – the recipe here makes enough seasoning for two batches.
I cook mine in the base of the air fryer, removing the tray or basket to do so. If you cannot do this, cook in a heatproof dish.

SERVES 4

2 tablespoons Fajita Seasoning (see below)

4 tablespoons extra virgin olive oil

800g (1lb 12oz) boneless, skinless chicken thighs, quartered

1 yellow pepper, cored, deseeded and sliced

1 red pepper, cored, deseeded and sliced

2 red onions, cut into 6 wedges each

1 courgette, cut into 6 x batons, each 1.5cm (⅝ inch) long

4 tortillas

lime wedges, to serve

FOR THE GUACAMOLE

flesh of 2 ripe avocados, mashed

5g (⅛oz) fresh coriander, stems and leaves, chopped

70g (2½oz) red onion, finely diced

½ tablespoon lime juice

1 plum tomato, peeled, deseeded and chopped

3 tablespoons extra virgin olive oil

salt and pepper

FOR THE FAJITA SEASONING

3 teaspoons mild chilli powder

2 teaspoons ground cumin

2 teaspoons sweet smoked paprika

2 teaspoons unrefined sugar

1½ teaspoons salt

¾ teaspoon onion powder

1 teaspoon garlic powder

¼ teaspoon cayenne pepper

Preheat the air fryer to 180°C (350°F).

Mix all the fajita seasoning ingredients together in a bowl, then transfer to an airtight container or jar.

Place 2 tablespoons of the seasoning in a large mixing bowl with the olive oil, chicken and vegetables and toss to coat.

Cook the chicken in a single layer in the air fryer for 30 minutes, or until the chicken is cooked through (if you have a meat thermometer, the internal temperature should be 74°C/165°F).

Meanwhile, mix all the guacamole ingredients together in a separate bowl and season to taste.

Serve the chicken and veg mixture on the tortillas with the guacamole, and wedges of lime for squeezing over.

CHICKEN PARMESAN

This dish uses a basic tomato sauce which I always have ready in the freezer in batches (see page 10). That's because I realized quite quickly when reviewing ready-made pasta sauces that many (in fact the majority) contain UPF ingredients. If you have a smaller air fryer, you might need to cook this recipe in two batches.

SERVES 4

75g (2¾oz) plain flour

2 large eggs, beaten

75g (2¾oz) fresh breadcrumbs

⅛ teaspoon pepper

50g (1¾oz) Parmesan cheese, finely grated

4 boneless, skinless chicken breasts, about 150g (5½oz) each, halved lengthways

660ml (1 pint 2fl oz) Ubiquitous Tomato Sauce (see page 10)

225g (8oz) mozzarella, drained and roughly torn

salt

Preheat the air fryer to 180°C (350°F).

Place the flour in a shallow bowl and season with salt. Place the beaten eggs in a second bowl, then combine the breadcrumbs, pepper and grated Parmesan in a third bowl. Dip each chicken piece first into the flour, then the egg, then the Parmesan breadcrumbs to coat all over.

Cook the breaded chicken breast pieces in the air fryer for 15–20 minutes, turning once, or until cooked through (if you have a meat thermometer, the internal temperature should be 74°C/165°F).

Pour the tomato sauce into a deep heatproof dish that fits in the air fryer. Heat in the air fryer for 3 minutes, stirring once, until warmed through.

Arrange the chicken pieces on top of the sauce, then arrange the mozzarella on top of the chicken. Cook for a further 4 minutes, until melted, then serve.

STUFFED TOMATOES

This is a great recipe for using up ripe summer tomatoes. They really do have a peak season when they're at their ripest and most nutritious, despite being in supermarkets all year round. Stuffed tomatoes can be enjoyed as a main, or they make the perfect side dish to accompany Stuffed Courgettes (see page 62), or as a side dish with Peri-Peri Chicken (see page 128).

**SERVES 2
AS A MAIN
OR 4 AS A SIDE**

4 tomatoes, about 130g (4¾oz) each

1 garlic clove, finely chopped

2 tablespoons chopped parsley

2 tablespoons chopped basil

1 teaspoon chopped thyme

2 tablespoons finely grated Parmesan cheese

35g (1¼oz) fresh breadcrumbs

1 teaspoon olive oil

salt and pepper

Preheat the air fryer to 170°C (340°F).

Slice the tops off the tomatoes, then scoop out and discard the seeds. Season the insides with salt and place in a heatproof dish that fits in the air fryer.

Blitz the garlic, herbs, Parmesan, breadcrumbs and seasoning in a food processor until all the ingredients are very finely chopped and well mixed. Alternatively, chop them finely and mix together by hand. Evenly divide this mixture between the tomatoes and then pop their tops back on.

Drizzle over the olive oil, then cook in the air fryer for 15–18 minutes, until the tomatoes are cooked.

HALLOUMI BAKED MUSHROOMS

Not only is halloumi delicious when air-fried in cubes or strips, you can also grate it as a topping for other air-fried foods. That's exactly what this recipe does – combines grated halloumi with cream cheese and sun-dried tomatoes as a filling for mushrooms. A powerful palate-pleaser.

SERVES 3

80g (2¾oz) halloumi, grated

80g (2¾oz) cream cheese

50g (1¾oz) sun-dried tomatoes, finely chopped

3 large flat mushrooms

Preheat the air fryer to 180°C (350°F).

Mix the halloumi, cream cheese and sun-dried tomatoes together in a bowl.

Wipe the mushrooms clean, then carefully remove and discard the stalks. Place the mushrooms gill sides up in a heatproof dish that fits in the air fryer, and divide the cheese mixture between them. Cook in the air fryer for 10 minutes, or until tender, before serving.

CREAMY MUSHROOM PASTA SAUCE

Jars of creamy pasta sauce commonly contain many ultra-processed ingredients, from modified maize starch and xanthan gum, to added flavourings and sweeteners. This creamy mushroom sauce is made from simple, real food ingredients. It uses frozen mushrooms which, when cooked in an air fryer, naturally release their moisture to create an umami-rich pasta sauce, here enhanced with cream, cheese and a little balsamic vinegar.

SERVES 2

- 300g (10½oz) frozen sliced mushrooms
- 1 teaspoon frozen chopped parsley
- 1 teaspoon frozen chopped garlic
- ½ teaspoon salt
- ¼ teaspoon pepper
- 1 teaspoon olive oil
- ½ teaspoon balsamic vinegar
- 150g (5½oz) dried pasta
- 50g (1¾oz) Parmesan cheese, finely grated, plus extra to serve
- 5 tablespoons double cream

Preheat the air fryer to 180°C (350°F).

Place the mushrooms, parsley, garlic, salt, pepper, olive oil and vinegar in a heatproof dish that fits in the air fryer. Cook in the air fryer for 10 minutes, stirring once, or until the mushrooms release their liquid and are soft.

Meanwhile, cook the pasta according to the packet instructions.

Stir the Parmesan and cream into the sauce until the cheese has melted. Drain the pasta and return to the saucepan, pour over the mushroom sauce and heat gently until warmed through. Serve, sprinkled with a little extra grated Parmesan.

HALLOUMI & COURGETTE KEBABS

Halloumi has experienced a recent surge in popularity – not only can you buy it as a block of cheese, but also as ready-prepared kebabs with a variety of marinades, as breaded sticks and even as burgers – this is an opportunity for manufacturers to add ultra-processed ingredients. These kebabs combine halloumi with flavour-absorbing courgette slices, both marinated for an hour before cooking. They're lovely and simple, and a perfect accompaniment to the Mediterranean Veg & Couscous Salad on page 142. If you like things extra spicy, replace some of the olive oil with a teaspoon of chilli oil.

SERVES 2

½ red chilli, finely diced

1 tablespoon olive oil

1 courgette, cut into 1cm (½ inch) thick discs

250g (9oz) halloumi, cut into 12 cubes

1 teaspoon runny honey, plus extra to serve

2 tablespoons chopped mint

Put the chilli in a large bowl with the olive oil. Add the courgette and halloumi, toss together, then cover and leave to marinate for up to an hour.

Preheat the air fryer to 180°C (350°F).

Assemble the kebabs by threading alternate pieces of courgette and halloumi on to metal or soaked wooden skewers. Cook in the air fryer for 8–10 minutes, turning the skewers once and recoating with any leftover oil half way through. Sprinkle with the honey and chopped mint, and serve immediately with extra honey on the side.

LAMB KOFTA BURGERS
WITH TZATZIKI

An air fryer is a great way to cook burgers, leaving them moist yet cooking them quickly. Many shop-bought burgers contain breadcrumbs or flour, and often added flavourings and preservatives. This succulent burger recipe uses lamb and spices to contrast beautifully with the creamy, cooling tzatziki.

SERVES 4

500g (1lb 2oz) minced lamb

1 red onion, finely chopped

2 garlic cloves, finely chopped

1 teaspoon ground cumin

1 teaspoon ground coriander

2 tablespoons chopped parsley

¾ teaspoon salt

TZATZIKI

½ cucumber, peeled and finely diced

2 teaspoons white wine vinegar

pinch of salt

150g (5½oz) Greek yogurt

1 garlic clove, crushed

1 tablespoon chopped mint

TO SERVE

pittas or burger buns

salad

For the tzatziki, spread the cucumber dice out in a sieve and sprinkle over the vinegar and a pinch of salt. Leave to drain for an hour, then pat dry with kitchen paper. Mix with the rest of the tzatziki ingredients, then taste and adjust the seasoning if necessary. Pop this in the fridge while you make the burgers.

Preheat the air fryer to 180°C (350°F).

Combine all the burger ingredients well using a food processor or by hand. Mould the lamb mixture into 8 equal burgers, each about 7cm (2¾ inches) in diameter. Cook the burgers in a single layer in the air fryer for 4 minutes on each side (if you have a meat thermometer, the internal temperature should be 63°C/145°F). Cook in batches if necessary.

Serve the burgers and tzatziki in pittas or buns with salad.

BEEF MEATBALLS
FOR A FAMILY FEAST

This recipe makes deliciously moist meatballs, like those I used to eat as a child, and before ready-made ones were available in the supermarket, which these days commonly contain added preservatives, seasonings and sweeteners. The moisture comes from including fresh breadcrumbs and milk, just the way my mother used to do.

SERVES 4

60g (2¼oz) fresh breadcrumbs

125ml (4fl oz) whole milk or non-dairy substitute

500g (1lb 2oz) minced beef

2 eggs

1 onion, grated

1 garlic clove, crushed

1 teaspoon salt

1 teaspoon dried oregano

½ teaspoon pepper

330ml (11fl oz) Ubiquitous Tomato Sauce (see page 10), to serve

Preheat the air fryer to 180°C (350°F).

Soak the breadcrumbs in the milk for a few minutes until all the liquid has been absorbed.

Mix all the ingredients (except the tomato sauce) together in a large bowl, using your hands to combine well, then roll into 16 equal meatballs. Cook them in the air fryer in a single layer for for 13–15 minutes, or until cooked through (if you have a meat thermometer, the internal temperature should be over 71°C/160°F). If your air fryer is smaller, you may need to cook them in 2 batches.

Warm the tomato sauce if necessary and serve with the meatballs.

SQUASH, SAUSAGE & CRISPY KALE BAKE

Crispy kale provides a highly nutritious way to add texture to this deliciously sweet and savoury bake. Remember to check for UPF ingredients in the mustard before buying it. This bake is delicious served with Ratatouille (see page 141).

SERVES 2

125g (4½oz) butternut squash flesh, cut into 1cm (½ inch) cubes

125g (4½oz) red onion, cut into wedges

1 tablespoon extra virgin olive oil

¼ teaspoon salt

½ teaspoon dried thyme

8 UPF-free chipolatas

1½ teaspoons runny honey

1 teaspoon wholegrain mustard

FOR THE CRISPY KALE

30g (1oz) kale

½ teaspoon extra virgin olive oil

salt

Preheat the air fryer to 170°C (340°F).

For the crispy kale, rinse and dry the kale, then remove any thick stems. Toss with the olive oil and a little salt, then lay out the pieces in the air fryer and cover with a grill rack to stop them flying around during cooking. Cook for 1 minute, then turn and cook the other side for 1 minute. Remove from the air fryer and set aside,, then increase the heat to 180°C (350°F).

Toss the squash and onion in the olive oil, salt and thyme. Place in a heatproof dish that fits in the air fryer and cook for 8 minutes, stirring once. If you have a smaller air fryer, you may need to do this in batches.

Meanwhile, toss the chipolatas in the honey and mustard and then place on top of the vegetables. Cook for a further 12 minutes, giving everything a good stir half way through, or until the sausages are cooked through (if you have a meat thermometer, the internal temperature should be 71°C/160°F). Serve with the crispy kale on top.

STUFFED COURGETTES

Courgettes are sometimes considered to be a fairly boring vegetable. However, scooping out their flavour-absorbing flesh and cooking them alongside some classic Mediterranean vegetables heightens their appeal to another level. This combination makes a wonderful, seasonal dish which can be served as a main in its own right, as a side dish together with the Stuffed Tomatoes (see page 50), or as an accompaniment to the Cod Wrapped in Parma Ham (see page 102).

SERVES 2
*AS A MAIN
OR 4 AS A SIDE*

1 tablespoon extra virgin olive oil

1 small onion, finely chopped

1 garlic clove, finely chopped

2 courgettes, cut in half lengthways

1 plum tomato, deseeded and chopped

½ red pepper, cored, deseeded and chopped

¼ teaspoon salt

⅛ teaspoon pepper

80g (2¾oz) Parmesan cheese

In a saucepan, heat the olive oil over a medium heat. Add the onion and garlic and sauté for 5 minutes. Meanwhile, scoop out the insides of the courgettes using a metal spoon, leaving the structure intact to fill later – I find a serrated spoon makes this even easier. Scrape out as much of the flesh as you can without damaging the skin, then chop it finely.

Add the tomato and red pepper to the onion saucepan with the courgette flesh, salt and pepper. Sauté for a further 5 minutes to reduce some of the liquid. Finely grate three-quarters of the Parmesan, stir it in and then remove from the heat.

Preheat the air fryer to 170°C (340°F).

Pop the courgette halves, cut sides up, on to a baking sheet that fits the air fryer. You may need to cook the courgettes in 2 batches if you have a smaller air fryer. Fill each courgette half with some vegetables, shave the remaining Parmesan over the top and cook in the air fryer for 12 minutes. Remove and serve immediately.

PORK & HOISIN MEATBALLS

Shop-bought hoisin sauce is often thickened with UPFs and sometimes flavoured with them too. This homemade sauce flavours deliciously spiced and moist pork meatballs which go well with a vegetable stir-fry.

SERVES 3–4

2 tablespoons soy sauce

1 tablespoon peanut butter (smooth or crunchy)

2 teaspoons runny honey

1 teaspoon rice wine vinegar

½ teaspoon Chinese five spice powder

500g (1lb 2oz) minced pork

2 teaspoons finely chopped garlic

Preheat the air fryer to 180°C (350°F).

Mix the soy sauce, peanut butter, honey, vinegar and five spice in a bowl. Transfer half the sauce mixture to a large bowl, add the minced pork and chopped garlic and mix well. Roll into 12 equal meatballs.

Cook the meatballs in the air fryer in a single layer for 7 minutes, then use a pastry brush to glaze them with the remaining sauce. Cook for a further 8 minutes, or until cooked through (if you have a meat thermometer, the internal temperature should be over 71°C/160°F).

CHORIZO & PORK BURGERS

Chorizo should be made from just pork, pork fat, garlic, salt and smoked paprika. Many shop-bought versions contain nitrates and nitrites as preservatives, and may also contain other added ingredients too, so check the labels to find one made in the traditional way. This recipe combines this delicious, traditional Spanish sausage with minced pork, tomato purée and oregano, for succulent and tasty burgers that are great with the Stuffed Courgettes on page 62.

SERVES 4

200g (7oz) traditional chorizo sausages

500g (1lb 2oz) minced pork

1 tablespoon tomato purée

1 teaspoon dried oregano

Preheat the air fryer to 180°C (350°F).

Peel the casings off the chorizo sausages, chop the meat finely and place in a bowl.

Mix in the minced pork, tomato purée and oregano, then form the mixture into 8 burgers, each 5–6cm (2–2½ inches) in diameter.

Cook the burgers in a single layer in the air fryer for 10–12 minutes, or until cooked through (if you have a meat thermometer, the internal temperature should be over 71°C/160°F). Cook in batches if necessary.

COMFORT FOOD

CHEAT'S CHICKEN KYIV

If you love chicken Kyiv but don't like the sound of some of the extracts and powders used to coat the chicken in shop-bought versions, this could be the recipe for you. Many a chicken Kyiv lover will have tried to make their own at home – it's quite a tricky process and often ends up with the garlic butter escaping before you've finished cooking the chicken, let alone getting it on to your plate. This much simpler recipe works well alongside the Roasted Tomatoes with Torn Mozzarella on page 79.

SERVES 4

60g (2¼oz) plain flour

½ teaspoon salt

¼ teaspoon pepper

2 eggs, beaten

100g (3½oz) fresh breadcrumbs

30g (1oz) Parmesan cheese, finely grated

4 boneless, skinless chicken breasts

1 quantity of Garlic Butter (see page 11)

Preheat the air fryer to 180°C (350°F).

Place the flour, salt and pepper in a shallow bowl and mix. Place the beaten eggs in a second bowl. Combine the breadcrumbs and Parmesan in a third bowl.

Place the chicken breasts, one at a time, between 2 sheets of clingfilm or greaseproof paper and flatten with a rolling pin until roughly 2cm (¾ inch) thick.

One at a time, dip each chicken breast into the seasoned flour, then into the egg and finally the breadcrumbs to coat. Cook the coated chicken breasts in a single layer in the air fryer for 20–25 minutes, turning once, or until cooked through (if you have a meat thermometer, the internal temperature should be 74°C/165°F). Melt one-quarter of the garlic butter over the top of each breast to serve.

CHICKEN STIR-FRY

There is an abundance of ready-to-use stir-fry sauces on the market that contain flavour enhancers and added starch. The marinade used in this recipe makes for a deliciously moist, authentic-tasting stir-fry without processed additives.

SERVES 2

2 tablespoons soy sauce

1 tablespoon UPF-free sriracha

1 teaspoon (peeled) chopped fresh root ginger

1 teaspoon chopped garlic

2 boneless, skinless chicken breasts, cut into bitesized cubes

1 tablespoon olive oil

1 onion, diced

8 chestnut mushrooms, sliced

1 red pepper, cored, deseeded and finely sliced

1 spring onion, chopped

steamed rice, to serve

Place the soy sauce, sriracha, ginger and garlic in a bowl and stir to combine. Add the chicken, stir well and set aside for 5 minutes.

Preheat the air fryer to 180°C (350°F).

Place the olive oil in the base of the air fryer (without the grill in place), then add the chicken and vegetables. Cook for 15–18 minutes, stirring from time to time during cooking, until the chicken is cooked through (if you have a meat thermometer, the internal temperature should be 74°C/165°F). Serve with steamed rice.

FISH FINGERS

Most commonly available in the freezer aisle of your supermarket, fish fingers tend to contain a range of additives to make for an even, crispy coating. This recipe for succulent, homemade fish fingers uses simply flour, eggs and breadcrumbs to create a crunchy, crispy coating. If you can find UPF-free olive oil in a spray bottle, it will be ideal for coating the fingers before cooking. Ideally serve with homemade Tartare Sauce (see page 11) to avoid further additives.

SERVES 2

40g (1½oz) plain flour

½ teaspoon salt

1 egg, beaten

60g (2¼oz) fresh
   breadcrumbs

250g (9oz) skinless
   cod fillet, cut into
   8 fingers

olive oil, for drizzling

TO SERVE

minted peas

new potatoes

Tartare Sauce (see
   page 11)

lemon wedges

Preheat the air fryer to 200°C (400°F).

Place the flour and salt in a shallow bowl and mix. Place the beaten egg in a second bowl and the breadcrumbs in a third.

Dip each fish finger into the seasoned flour, then the egg, then the breadcrumbs to coat. Drizzle (or spray) the fish fingers with olive oil, then cook in a single layer in the air fryer for 7 minutes, or until the fish just flakes.

Serve with minted peas and new potatoes, with homemade tartare sauce on the side and lemon wedges for squeezing over.

GNOCCHI BAKE

Many a pasta bake bought from stores will contain ultra-processed ingredients. With this comforting dish you can recognize all of the constituent ingredients. This is ideal for a quick, filling and comforting midweek meal.

SERVES 2

2 red peppers, cored, deseeded and roughly chopped

1 teaspoon extra virgin olive oil

330ml (11fl oz) Ubiquitous Tomato Sauce (see page 10)

400g (14oz) gnocchi

70g (2½oz) Parma ham, roughly torn

2 tablespoons finely grated Parmesan cheese

125g (4½oz) mozzarella, well drained and roughly torn

salt

Preheat the air fryer to 190°C (375°F).

Toss the peppers in the olive oil and ¼ teaspoon of salt in a heatproof dish that fits in the air fryer. Cook in the air fryer for 10 minutes. You may need to cook this in 2 batches, depending on the size of your air fryer.

Meanwhile, bring a saucepan of salted water to the boil on the hob.

Once the peppers have been cooking for 10 minutes, stir in the tomato sauce and cook for a further 2 minutes. Pop the gnocchi into the saucepan and cook according to the packet instructions.

Drain the gnocchi, add to the dish in the air fryer, stir well, then top with the Parma ham, grated Parmesan and mozzarella. Cook for a further 5 minutes, until piping hot.

TUNA PASTA BAKE

A family favourite! The list of ingredients for many pasta bakes can be as long as your arm; this ingredients list could almost be counted on one hand.

250g (9oz) pasta shapes, such as penne

330ml (11fl oz) Ubiquitous Tomato Sauce (see page 10)

145g (5¼oz) can tuna, drained

50g (1¾oz) frozen or canned sweetcorn

50g (1¾oz) pitted black olives, halved

50g (1¾oz) Parmesan cheese, finely grated

Cook the pasta according to the packet instructions.

Preheat the air fryer to 180°C (350°F).

Drain the pasta and return to the saucepan. Add the tomato sauce and stir to heat through. Add the tuna, sweetcorn and olives, stir to combine all the ingredients, then transfer to a heatproof dish that fits in the air fryer. Top with the Parmesan and cook in the air fryer for 6–8 minutes, or until piping hot throughout.

TWICE-BAKED CHEESY POTATOES

Here's an elevated version of the humble cheesy baked potato. Unbelievably (to me, anyway) you can buy pre-baked potatoes – and even ones with a cheese filling – in both the fresh and frozen aisles of the supermarket now. This version is made from simple, recognizable ingredients and tastes delicious with very little effort.

SERVES 2

2 baking potatoes

1 teaspoon extra virgin olive oil

½ teaspoon salt

15g (½oz) butter

50g (1¾oz) Red Leicester cheese, grated

pinch of chilli flakes

2 spring onions, finely sliced

Preheat the air fryer to 190°C (375°F).

Prick the potatoes with a fork, then rub the skins with the olive oil and salt. Cook in the air fryer for 45–50 minutes, or until they just give when a fork is inserted.

Leave to cool a little, then cut the potatoes in half and scrape out the flesh, leaving the skins intact. In a bowl, mash the potato flesh with the butter, half the grated cheese, the chilli flakes and spring onions.

Refill the potato skins with the potato and cheese mixture and top with the remaining cheese. Cook in the air fryer for a further 10 minutes. If your air fryer has a grill function, grill the cheese for the last few minutes for an even browner, crispier topping.

ROASTED TOMATOES
WITH TORN MOZZARELLA

These simple ingredients, when combined, make for a delicious dish. This goes well with the Cheat's Chicken Kyiv on page 69, or serve on top of the Garlic Ciabatta on page 101.

SERVES 2

500g (1lb 2oz) cherry tomatoes

2 tablespoons extra virgin olive oil

1 tablespoon balsamic vinegar

½ teaspoon salt

¼ teaspoon pepper

2 whole garlic cloves, peeled

200g (7oz) mozzarella, drained and roughly torn

3 tablespoons chopped basil

Preheat the air fryer to 180°C (350°F).

Place the tomatoes in a bowl and combine with the olive oil, vinegar, salt, pepper and garlic. Tip into a heatproof dish that fits in the air fryer, then cook in the air fryer for 12 minutes, stirring once half way through.

Crush the cooked garlic cloves with the back of a spoon, then stir into the dish. Stir in the mozzarella and basil just before serving.

UPF-FREE SCOTCH EGGS

A picnic classic, though these days hard to find without some UPF ingredients, including flavourings and starches. This homemade version allows you to control the ingredients and cook your eggs with a runny yolk (if that's to your liking). Choose UPF-free sausages – there are many on the market now, just seek those without preservatives.

4 eggs

400g (14oz) UPF-free sausages, skins removed

40g (1½oz) plain flour

¼ teaspoon salt

¼ teaspoon pepper

60g (2¼oz) fresh breadcrumbs

Carefully place 3 of the eggs in the air fryer and cook for 6 minutes (for soft-boiled) or 10 minutes (for hard-boiled), carefully remove the eggs from the air fryer using an oven mitt and place in a bowl of ice-cold water to cool. Peel carefully.

Meanwhile, divide the sausagemeat into 3 equal portions and flatten into discs with your hands. Place each peeled egg in the centre of a disc of sausagemeat and carefully roll into a ball, using a pinching action to close the sausagemeat around the egg.

Place the flour, salt and pepper in a shallow bowl and mix. Beat the remaining egg in a second bowl and place the breadcrumbs in a third.

Roll each Scotch egg in the seasoned flour, then the beaten egg and finally the breadcrumbs to coat. Pop them in the air fryer and set the cooking temperature to 180°C (350°F). Cook for 15 minutes, using the preheat time as part of the cooking time. Leave to cool a little, then slice and enjoy.

SWEET POTATO HASH
WITH PEANUT & MAPLE DRESSING

A rich and fruity dressing enlivens this delicious combination of onion, garlic and sweet potato, all roasted together in the air fryer.

SERVES 2
AS A SIDE

1 small onion, cut into 6 wedges

200g (7oz) sweet potato, unpeeled, scrubbed and cut into 2cm (¾ inch) cubes

1 tablespoon extra virgin olive oil

¼ teaspoon salt

¼ teaspoon garlic powder

½ teaspoon paprika

1 small head of garlic

2 fried eggs, to serve (optional)

FOR THE DRESSING

1 tablespoon smooth peanut butter

1 teaspoon warm water

1 teaspoon maple syrup

½ teaspoon lime juice

½ teaspoon soy sauce

Preheat the air fryer to 180°C (350°F).

Place the onion and sweet potato in a bowl with the olive oil and seasonings and mix well to coat. Transfer to a heatproof dish that fits in the air fryer. Slice the top off the head of garlic to reveal the tops of the cloves, then nestle it in among the vegetables. Cook in the air fryer for 20 minutes, stirring a couple of times during cooking, or until tender.

Meanwhile, make the dressing. Put the peanut butter in a small bowl and stir in the warm water to melt it a little. Add the maple syrup, lime juice and soy sauce and stir well.

When the vegetables are just cool enough to handle, squeeze the garlic flesh out of the skins and mix with the other vegetables. Drizzle over the dressing before serving. I like to serve this with a fried egg.

TACO-STUFFED SWEET POTATOES

Both taco and fajita packet seasonings tend to contain added UPF ingredients. This recipe uses a combination of simple spices from your cupboard to great effect to deliver on flavour. The spiced beef is served inside baked sweet potatoes with a quick and easy homemade guacamole on the side.

SERVES 4

4 sweet potatoes

½ teaspoon chilli powder

½ teaspoon ground cumin

½ teaspoon dried oregano

½ teaspoon salt

¼ teaspoon pepper

400g (14oz) minced beef

125g (4½oz) Red Leicester cheese, grated

125g (4½oz) soured cream

Guacamole (see page 46), to serve

Preheat the air fryer to 180°C (350°F).

Prick the sweet potato skins, place them in the air fryer and cook for 30–35 minutes, or until they just give when a fork is inserted.

Meanwhile, combine the chilli powder, cumin, oregano, salt and pepper in a small bowl. Heat a large frying pan over a medium heat, add the minced beef and the spice mix and cook until the meat is browned all over, breaking it up as you go – this should take 5–10 minutes.

Slice open the potatoes and fill with the beef mixture, then top with the grated cheese. Cook in the air fryer for a further 5 minutes, or until the cheese has just melted. You may need to cook in batches if you have a smaller air fryer. Top the potatoes with dollops of soured cream and serve with guacamole.

WHIPPED FETA-FILLED SWEET POTATOES

Salty, tangy and creamy, this whipped feta is the ideal filling for an air-fryer sweet potato. Although you can buy ready-made whipped feta in stores, it is often thickened with mayonnaise and some form of starch, and tends to have a lot of added ultra-processed ingredients including stabilizers, preservatives, firming agents and sometimes added sugar too.

SERVES 2

2 sweet potatoes

200g (7oz) feta

150g (5½oz) Greek yogurt

grated zest of ½ lemon

2 tablespoons olive oil

runny honey, for drizzling

15g (½oz) pomegranate seeds, for sprinkling

mixed leaf salad, to serve (optional)

Preheat the air fryer to 180°C (350°F).

Prick the sweet potato skins, place them in the air fryer and cook for 30–35 minutes, or until they just give when a fork is inserted.

To make the whipped feta, place the feta, yogurt, lemon zest and olive oil in a food processor and combine on a low-medium speed. You must be patient with this process as you want a smooth, thick and creamy consistency, and it does take time to achieve this.

Slice open the potatoes and top with the whipped feta, a drizzle of honey and some pomegranate seeds. Serve with a mixed leaf salad, if you like.

CREAMY MUSHROOMS ON TOAST

Mushrooms are a fantastic source of umami, which is one of the five basic tastes alongside sweet, salty, sour and bitter. 'Umami' is a Japanese word meaning 'delicious' and 'savoury'. This taste sensation is primarily due to the presence of glutamate, an amino acid found in high levels in mushrooms. Glutamate is often found in the form of ultra-processed monosodium glutamate (MSG) in processed foods, but these mushrooms provide a natural hit.

SERVES 2

200g (7oz) mushrooms, sliced

¼ teaspoon salt

1 tablespoon extra virgin olive oil

2 tablespoons finely grated Parmesan cheese

100ml (3½fl oz) double cream

2 tablespoons chopped parsley

toast, to serve

Preheat the air fryer to 170°C (340°F).

In a bowl, toss the mushrooms, salt and olive oil together, then transfer to a heatproof dish that fits in the air fryer. Cook in the air fryer for 8 minutes, stirring once during cooking.

Stir in the cheese, cream and parsley and cook for 1 further minute. Stir, then serve on toast.

AUBERGINE PARMESAN

These crispy coated aubergine slices topped with homemade tomato sauce and fresh mozzarella make a perfect side for a healthy lunch or evening meal.

SERVES 4
AS A SIDE

70g (2½oz) fresh sourdough breadcrumbs

30g (1oz) Parmesan cheese, finely grated

½ teaspoon dried oregano

¼ teaspoon salt

1 aubergine, about 300g (10½oz), cut into 1cm (½ inch) slices

250ml (9fl oz) Ubiquitous Tomato Sauce (see page 10)

125g (4½oz) mozzarella, drained and roughly torn

2 tablespoons chopped basil

FOR THE BATTER

1 large egg

2 tablespoons plain flour

salt

Preheat the air fryer to 180°C (350°F).

Mix the batter in a shallow bowl by whisking the egg and flour with a pinch of salt.

Mix the breadcrumbs in a second bowl with the Parmesan, oregano and salt. Dip the aubergine slices first in the batter, then in the crumb to coat all over. You will need to push the breadcrumbs on to the aubergine slices to ensure they stick well.

Cook the coated aubergine slices in the air fryer, in batches if necessary, for 12 minutes, turning half way through. Top each slice with about 1 tablespoon of the tomato sauce and some of the mozzarella. Cook for a further 3 minutes, then serve sprinkled with the basil.

EATING WITH
FRIENDS

BAKED BUTTERNUT SQUASH

Sweet and tender roasted butternut contrasts so well with the salty tanginess of blue cheese. The nuts bring great texture and a delicious crunch to the dish. I like to serve this with a green salad.

1 teaspoon extra virgin olive oil

700g (1lb 9oz) butternut squash, halved and deseeded

30g (1oz) unsalted butter

2 plump garlic cloves

50g (1¾oz) walnuts, chopped

100g (3½oz) blue cheese, crumbled

1 teaspoon chopped thyme

1½ teaspoons runny honey

Preheat the air fryer to 170°C (340°F).

Drizzle the olive oil over the squash halves and rub it in, then divide the butter between the 2 cavities. Cook flesh side up in the air fryer for 30 minutes, with the unpeeled garlic cloves alongside, or until soft all the way through when pierced with a fork.

Allow to cool a little, then scoop the butternut flesh into a bowl, leaving a 1cm (½ inch) layer attached to the skin. Squeeze the garlic flesh into the bowl with the squash.

Mash the squash and garlic with the nuts, cheese, thyme and honey, then divide this filling between the 2 squash halves. Return to the air fryer for 8 minutes before serving.

BEEF & CHORIZO MEATBALLS
IN MEDITERRANEAN SAUCE

Many people have said to me over the years that they cook the same dishes over and over in their air fryer. Finding out that they can cook many of the same dishes they would in their oven opens up a whole raft of tasty opportunities.

SERVES 4

1 red pepper, cored, deseeded and cut into 1cm (½ inch) strips

1 orange or yellow pepper, cored, deseeded and cut into 1cm (½ inch) strips

½ teaspoon salt

2 teaspoons olive oil

1 onion, finely chopped

1 garlic clove, finely chopped

400g (14oz) passata

1 teaspoon dried oregano

1 tablespoon tomato purée

1 teaspoon garlic salt

½ teaspoon runny honey

100g (3½oz) nitrate-free chorizo, finely chopped

400g (14oz) minced beef

Preheat the air fryer to 160°C (325°F).

Place the peppers in a roasting tin that fits in the air fryer, sprinkle over the salt and drizzle over the olive oil. Cook in the air fryer for 12 minutes, or until colouring at the edges.

If you have a smaller air fryer, you may have to cook this in batches or halve the recipe.

Meanwhile, blitz the onion and garlic in a mini food processor before mixing with the passata, dried oregano, tomato purée, garlic salt and honey.

Mix the chorizo with the minced beef and roll the mixture into 12 equal meatballs.

Pour the sauce over the peppers and add the meatballs to the tin. Cover with foil and cook for 15 minutes, then remove the foil and cook in the air fryer for a further 15 minutes, or until the meatballs are just cooked through but still moist (if you have a meat thermometer, the internal temperature should be 74°C/165°F).

BEEF NACHOS

Who doesn't love a tray of hearty nachos? Everything is made from scratch in this simple but substantial recipe.

½ teaspoon chilli powder

½ teaspoon ground cumin

½ teaspoon dried oregano

½ teaspoon salt

¼ teaspoon pepper

400g (14oz) minced beef

300g (10½oz) lightly salted tortilla chips

160g (5¾oz) Cheddar cheese, grated

2 tomatoes, deseeded and diced

½ red pepper, cored, deseeded and diced

150g (5½oz) soured cream

1 spring onion, very thinly sliced

Preheat the air fryer to 160°C (325°F).

Combine the chilli powder, cumin, oregano, salt and pepper in a small bowl. Heat a large frying pan over a medium heat and cook the minced beef and spices for 5–10 minutes, or until the meat is browned all over, breaking up the beef as you go.

Arrange half the tortilla chips in the base of the air fryer drawer or in a deep heatproof dish that fits in the air fryer. Top with half the cheese, half the beef and half the tomato and red pepper. Repeat the layers to use the remaining ingredients, then pop into the air fryer for 5 minutes. Serve with the soured cream and spring onion on top.

BEETROOT & FETA TARTS

A classic combination of flavours – beetroot, caramelized onions and feta – on a beautifully crisp pastry base. Ready-made pastry often contains additives, so seek out those labelled 'all butter' for the least-processed option.

1 sheet of ready-rolled all-butter puff pastry

50g (1¾oz) walnuts

1 egg, beaten

200g (7oz) feta, cut into 2cm (¾ inch) cubes

200g (7oz) cooked beetroot, cut into 2cm (¾ inch) cubes

½ teaspoon dried thyme

FOR THE CARAMELIZED RED ONIONS

1 teaspoon olive oil

200g (7oz) red onions, thinly sliced

1 tablespoon butter

¼ teaspoon salt

1½ teaspoons maple syrup

For the caramelized red onions, heat the olive oil in a small saucepan over a medium heat. Add the onions and butter and sauté until the onions start to soften. Add the salt and maple syrup and reduce the heat to low. Cook for 10–12 minutes until the onions are reduced and jammy in appearance, adding a little water if the onions become dry. Leave to cool.

Remove the pastry from the fridge 10 minutes before you start preparing this dish to reduce the chance of it cracking.

Preheat the air fryer to 180°C (350°F).

Place the walnuts in a heatproof dish that fits in the air fryer. Cook in the air fryer for 2–3 minutes, turning once, or until toasted. Leave to cool a little, then roughly chop. Meanwhile, cut the pastry into 4 rectangles, each about 15 x 10cm (6 x 4 inches). Score a line around the edge of each rectangle of pastry 1cm (½ inch) in from the sides, being careful not to cut into the pastry. Brush the beaten egg around the border of each rectangle to create a crust around the tarts. Cook the pastry rectangles in the air fryer for 5 minutes. Depending on the size of your air fryer, you may need to do this in batches.

Divide the caramelized onions, the feta and beetroot between the partially-cooked pastry bases, then carefully brush the top of the feta and beetroot with a little beaten egg. Sprinkle with the thyme and cook for a further 8 minutes, or until the tarts are golden brown. Scatter over the chopped toasted walnuts and serve.

BRUSCHETTA

Easy to throw together and made from simple ingredients, this straightforward recipe harnesses the natural sweetness of tomatoes, combining them with the classic flavours of balsamic vinegar, basil and garlic. This recipe can easily be scaled up to serve more people.

6 vine tomatoes, deseeded and diced

2 tablespoons roughly torn basil

½ teaspoon balsamic vinegar

4 teaspoons extra virgin olive oil

2 garlic cloves, peeled

2 slices of sourdough bread

salt and pepper

Preheat the air fryer to 200°C (400°F).

Place the tomatoes, basil, balsamic vinegar and half the olive oil in a bowl and season to taste. Finely chop one garlic clove, add it to the bowl and stir well.

Rub both sides of each slice of bread with the other (halved) garlic clove, then brush with the remaining olive oil. Cook the bread in the air fryer for 2 minutes on each side until toasted and golden. Serve with the tomato mixture on top.

GARLIC CIABATTA

Garlic bread is a popular choice for many, yet it often contains emulsifiers and flavourings. This recipe uses real, recognizable ingredients.

180g (6¼oz) ciabatta, halved, or 2 ciabatta rolls

1½ tablespoons Garlic Butter (see page 11), at room temperature

1 teaspoon frozen chopped parsley

1 teaspoon extra virgin olive oil

salt

Preheat the air fryer to 200°C (400°F).

Slice the ciabatta bread or rolls in half horizontally, then spread the cut sides with the garlic butter. Sprinkle over the parsley, olive oil and some salt. Cook in the air fryer, cut sides up, for 4 minutes. Serve as soon as it is cool enough to handle.

COD WRAPPED IN PARMA HAM

This dish is so easy and quick, yet the results are worthy of a dinner party. Roasted Tomatoes with Torn Mozzarella (see page 79) makes a great accompaniment.

6 slices of Parma ham

2 skinless cod fillets, about 130g (4¾oz) each

2 heaped teaspoons UPF-free pesto

rocket leaves, to serve (optional)

Preheat the air fryer to 180°C (350°F).

Lay 3 slices of Parma ham out on a chopping board with the edges slightly overlapping. Repeat with the other 3 slices. Place a cod fillet on top of each and top with the pesto, spreading it over the fish. Wrap the ham around the cod, covering it as completely as possible.

Cook the fish in a single layer in the air fryer for 10 minutes, or until cooked through (if you have a meat thermometer, the internal temperature should be 63°C/145°F). Serve with a rocket salad, if you like.

HALLOUMI CAESAR SALAD

This homemade Caesar salad dressing is free from UPFs and utterly delicious.

250g (9oz) halloumi, cut into 2cm (¾ inch) thick pieces

1 teaspoon extra virgin olive oil

1 large Romaine lettuce heart, about 175g (6oz)

1 tablespoon finely grated Parmesan cheese

FOR THE DRESSING

30g (1oz) Parmesan cheese, finely grated

50g (1¾oz) UPF-free mayonnaise

2 tablespoons milk

1 tablespoon lemon juice

1 teaspoon Dijon mustard

FOR THE CROÛTONS

110g (3¾oz) rustic bread, cut into 2cm (¾ inch) cubes

1 tablespoon extra virgin olive oil

pinch of salt

Preheat the air fryer to 180°C (350°F).

Make the dressing by combining all the dressing ingredients in a bowl.

For the croûtons, toss the bread in a bowl with the olive oil and salt. Cook in the air fryer for 2 minutes, then shake the basket and cook for a further 2 minutes, or until crispy. Remove the croûtons and increase the temperature of the air fryer to 190°C (375°F).

Brush the halloumi slices all over with the olive oil, then cook in the air fryer in a single layer for 8–10 minutes, or until crispy on the outside, turning once during cooking.

Toss the lettuce leaves in the dressing and arrange on a platter, then top with the croûtons and halloumi and sprinkle with the grated Parmesan.

SWEET POTATO, BLUE CHEESE & WALNUT SALAD

A feast for both the eyes and the taste buds. The sweet potatoes are roasted to perfection providing a warm, sweet contrast to the tangy blue cheese. The air fryer really accentuates the toasted flavour of the crunchy walnuts, too.

**SERVES 2
AS A SIDE**

1 sweet potato, peeled, halved and cut into 5mm (¼ inch) half moons

½ teaspoon ground sumac

1 teaspoon extra virgin olive oil

60g (2¼oz) walnuts, roughly chopped

60g (2¼oz) rocket leaves

2 tablespoons Vinaigrette Dressing (see page 11)

50g (1¾oz) crumbly blue cheese

salt and pepper

Preheat the air fryer to 180°C (350°F).

Place the sweet potato in a bowl with the sumac, olive oil and seasoning and toss to coat. Arrange in a single layer in the air fryer and cook for 12 minutes, or until it just gives when pierced with a fork. If you have a smaller air fryer, you may need to do this in batches. Add the walnuts to the air fryer and cook for a further 3 minutes.

Place the rocket, sweet potato and toasted walnuts in a bowl with half the dressing and toss gently to coat. Crumble the blue cheese on top and serve.

MISO SALMON
WITH BROCCOLI

Miso paste provides a rich savoury flavour to this tempting salmon dish, ideal for sharing with friends.

2 teaspoons UPF-free white miso paste

1 tablespoon sesame, avocado or olive oil

1 tablespoon soy sauce

1 tablespoon finely chopped (peeled) fresh root ginger

2 spring onions, finely chopped

4 skinless salmon fillets, about 130g (4¾oz) each

200g (7oz) Tenderstem broccoli

TO SERVE
parsley leaves
steamed rice
lime wedges

Place the miso, oil, soy sauce, chopped ginger and spring onions in a bowl and mix well.

Place the salmon and broccoli in a heatproof dish that fits in the air fryer and pour over the sauce over and chill in the fridge for at least 10 minutes, but ideally several hours.

Preheat the air fryer to 180°C (350°F).

Cook the salmon and broccoli in the air fryer for 10–12 minutes, or until the salmon is just cooked through (if you have a meat thermometer, the internal temperature of the fish should be 50°C/122°F).

Serve immediately with a scattering of parsley leaves, and steamed rice and lime wedges on the side.

FAKEAWAYS

CHICKEN TACOS
WITH TOMATO SALSA

With a simple, homemade marinade, these flavoursome chicken tacos make for the ultimate midweek fakeaway.

SERVES 4

500g (1lb 2oz) boneless, skinless chicken thighs

12 UPF-free mini tortilla wraps

flesh of 1 ripe avocado, diced

2 tablespoons chopped fresh coriander

4 tablespoons soured cream

lime wedges, for squeezing over

FOR THE MARINADE

1½ teaspoons lemon juice

1½ teaspoons extra virgin olive oil

¼ teaspoon chilli powder

½ teaspoon ground cumin

½ teaspoon paprika

½ teaspoon dried oregano

¼ teaspoon garlic powder

¼ teaspoon salt

FOR THE SALSA

3 tomatoes, peeled, deseeded and finely chopped

¼ red onion, very finely chopped

½ small garlic clove, very finely chopped

dash of white wine vinegar

squeeze of lime juice

1 tablespoon roughly chopped fresh coriander

Mix the marinade ingredients together in a large bowl. Add the chicken thighs, toss to coat, then cover and leave to marinate in the fridge overnight.

Preheat the air fryer to 180°C (350°F).

Cook the chicken in a single layer in the air fryer for 22–24 minutes, turning once during cooking, or until cooked through (if you have a meat thermometer, the internal temperature should be 74°C/165°F).

For the salsa, mix all the ingredients together in a bowl.

Roughly chop the cooked chicken and serve alongside the salsa, wraps, avocado, coriander and soured cream and with lime wedges for squeezing over.. Allow everyone to fill their own tacos with each of the different fillings.

CHICKEN TIKKA

Packs of ready-to-eat chicken tikka tend to contain starches, stabilizers and even sweeteners. Instead, make your own using a marinade of yogurt, lemon juice, spices and seasoning. The marinade is what gives the texture and flavour you'd expect from succulent chicken tikka, so allow time for those flavours to seep in. The cooking is the quick part.

SERVES 4

500g (1lb 2oz) boneless, skinless chicken breasts, cut into 3cm (1¼ inch) cubes

1 teaspoon melted butter

TO SERVE (OPTIONAL)

Greek yogurt

sliced red onion

fresh coriander leaves

lemon wedges

UPF-free flatbreads

FOR THE TIKKA MARINADE

1 tablespoon (peeled) grated fresh root ginger

1 tablespoon grated garlic

3 tablespoons Greek yogurt

½ teaspoon salt

1 teaspoon cayenne pepper

¼ teaspoon pepper

1 teaspoon paprika

1 teaspoon ground coriander

1 teaspoon lemon juice

1½ teaspoons gram flour

Combine all the marinade ingredients in a large bowl, toss in the chicken and coat well. Cover and chill in the fridge for at least 4 hours, ideally overnight.

Preheat the air fryer to 180°C (350°F).

Place the chicken in the air fryer in a single layer and brush the tops of the pieces with melted butter. Cook for 7 minutes, then turn over the pieces of chicken and brush the other sides with the remaining melted butter. Increase the temperature to 200°C (400°F) and cook for a further 5–7 minutes, or until cooked through (if you have a meat thermometer, the internal temperature should be 74°C/165°F).

Serve with Greek yogurt, sliced red onion, coriander leaves, flatbreads and lemon wedges for squeezing over, if you like.

JAPANESE-STYLE 'FRIED' CHICKEN

This recipe uses potato starch flour. Although not a normal store cupboard ingredient for many, it is great for creating the crispiness of deep-fat-fried foods without using UPF ingredients. Serve this crispy chicken with tangy pickled cucumber.

450g (1lb) boneless, skinless chicken thighs, cut into bite-sized pieces

2 tablespoons soy sauce

2 tablespoons mirin

1 teaspoon (peeled) grated fresh root ginger

1 teaspoon grated garlic

70g (2½oz) potato starch flour

FOR THE PICKLED CUCUMBER

½ cucumber

2 tablespoons Japanese rice vinegar

1½ teaspoons unrefined sugar

1 teaspoon grated fresh root (peeled) ginger

2 spring onions, finely chopped

Toss the chicken pieces in a bowl with the soy sauce, mirin, ginger and garlic, coating the chicken well. Cover, then place in the fridge for at least an hour, ideally overnight.

Meanwhile, for the pickled cucumber, cut the cucumber in half lengthways, then thinly slice it using a mandolin or sharp knife. Mix together the rice vinegar, sugar and ginger in a bowl, stir in the spring onions and cucumber, then cover and chill until ready to eat.

Preheat the air fryer to 180°C (350°F).

Arrange the marinated chicken pieces in a single layer on a chopping board. Shake over a layer of the potato starch flour using a sieve, then turn the chicken pieces over and coat the other sides in the same way. Shake the chicken pieces to remove any excess starch.

Cook the chicken in a single layer in the air fryer for 10 minutes, shaking the drawer once during cooking, or until cooked through (if you have a meat thermometer, the internal temperature should be 74°C/165°F). Serve the crispy chicken with the pickled cucumber.

DECONSTRUCTED PIZZA BURGERS

Compare a burger bun to an English muffin in most supermarkets and you'll find a far more real set of ingredients in the muffin. Pizzas and burgers are both synonymous with junk food, yet when their respective flavours and ingredients are combined from scratch, they make for a delicious combination. These pizza burgers, served on English muffins, are a real crowd-pleaser.

SERVES 4

1 tablespoon extra virgin olive oil

1 small red onion, finely chopped

500g (1lb 2oz) minced beef

¾ teaspoon dried oregano

¾ teaspoon dried basil

¾ teaspoon garlic powder

¾ teaspoon salt

330ml (11fl oz) Ubiquitous Tomato Sauce (see page 10)

4 English muffins, split

80g (2¾oz) cooking mozzarella, grated

TO SERVE

rocket leaves or a crisp green salad

Corn on the Cob (see page 135)

Heat the olive oil in a frying pan over a medium heat, then cook the onion for about 5 minutes until softened.

Add the minced beef, herbs, garlic powder and salt and fry until the beef is browned all over, breaking it up as you go. Add the tomato sauce, then cook on a low simmer for about 5 minutes.

Preheat the air fryer to 180°C (350°F).

Cook the muffin halves in the air fryer for 1 minute on each side, then remove.

Carefully divide the cooked beef mixture between the muffin halves, then scatter over the cheese. Arrange the muffin halves, in batches if necessary, directly on the air fryer rack, and cook, using the grill function if you have one, for 2–4 minutes, or until the tops of the muffins are browned. Serve with rocket leaves or a crisp green salad and corn on the cob.

FLATBREAD PIZZAS

These simple pizzas are ideal for lunches and picnics, but can also be served hot as a quick snack or tea for younger children. They can add their own toppings before the pizzas go into the air fryer.

100g (3½oz) passata

2 UPF-free flatbreads or tortilla wraps

½ teaspoon extra virgin olive oil

50g (1¾oz) hard cheese, such as Cheddar or Red Leicester, grated

½ teaspoon dried oregano

basil leaves, to garnish

tomato and red onion salad, to serve

Preheat the air fryer to 200°C (400°F).

Spread half the passata over each flatbread or tortilla, leaving a 1cm (½ inch) border around the edges. Use the olive oil to brush the border for a super-crispy crust.

Top the flatbreads/wraps with the cheese and oregano, then cook in the air fryer for 5 minutes, or until melted. You may need to do this in 2 batches, depending on the size of your air fryer.

Garnish with basil leaves and serve with a tomato and red onion salad.

GRILLED CHEESE SANDWICH

A classic comfort food. So simple and yet so satisfying; made from simple, real-food ingredients. Grilled cheese sandwiches often rely on processed cheese slices which invariably use multiple emulsifiers to give that melted, gooey texture.

SERVES 1

1 tablespoon butter

2 slices of rustic bread, such as sourdough

50g (1¾oz) Red Leicester or Cheddar cheese, thinly sliced

Preheat the air fryer to 180°C (350°F).

Butter the slices of bread on one side. Lay one slice, buttered side down, on a board and top with the cheese in an even layer. Top with the second bread slice, buttered side up, pushing it down firmly. Cook in the air fryer for 6–8 minutes, or until the bread is toasted and the cheese has melted.

NANDO'S-STYLE CHICKEN WINGS

Possibly one of the greatest benefits of an air fryer is recreating your favourite takeaway dishes, but using better, unprocessed ingredients. These wings are a perfect example.

1½ teaspoons lemon juice

1½ teaspoons extra virgin olive oil

¼ teaspoon chilli powder

½ teaspoon ground cumin

½ teaspoon paprika

½ teaspoon dried oregano

¼ teaspoon garlic powder

¼ teaspoon salt

500g (1lb 2oz) chicken wings

TO SERVE

chilli sauce

Greek yogurt

lemon wedges

Combine all the ingredients in a large bowl and toss to coat. Cover and chill in the fridge overnight.

Preheat the air fryer to 180°C (350°F).

Place the marinated chicken wings in the air fryer in a single layer and cook for 15–20 minutes, or until cooked through (if you have a meat thermometer, the internal temperature should be 74°C/165°F).

Serve with your favourite chilli sauce and some Greek yogurt for dipping, and lemon wedges for squeezing over.

ROTISSERIE POUSSIN

The rotisserie chickens you see in shops dripping with deliciously seasoned cooking juices are so appealing. Some shops even sell chickens ready to roast with the spices contained in the cooking bag. This recipe, however, makes for an unprocessed version, avoiding stabilizers, starches and flavourings. Poussins are simply small chickens, but they lend themselves well to this recipe as they stay moist on the inside but get crispier on the outside.

2 poussins

1 tablespoon butter

1 teaspoon paprika

1 teaspoon salt

1 teaspoon garlic powder

½ teaspoon dried thyme

⅛ teaspoon pepper

⅛ teaspoon cayenne pepper

TO SERVE

salad leaves

Vinaigrette Dressing (see page 11)

Preheat the air fryer to 180°C (350°F).

Rub the poussins all over with the butter. Mix together all the remaining ingredients, then rub this into the skin of each poussin.

Cook the poussins in the air fryer, breast sides up, for 15 minutes. Turn them and cook for a further 15 minutes, or until cooked through (if you have a meat thermometer, the internal temperature should be 74°C/165°F). Leave to rest for 10 minutes in the air fryer before serving with salad leaves and vinaigrette dressing.

PERI-PERI CHICKEN

These moist chicken thighs provide a delicate spiciness and warmth from the chilli and garlic. Many shop-bought peri peri marinades and spice mixes contain ingredients such as anti-caking agents and starches – this marinade does not.

SERVES 2

6 boneless, skinless chicken thighs

juice of 1 lemon

1 tablespoon extra virgin olive oil

1 teaspoon smoked paprika

½ teaspoon chilli flakes

2 garlic cloves, crushed

1 teaspoon dried oregano

1 tablespoon chopped parsley

½ teaspoon salt

¼ teaspoon pepper

TO SERVE

Corn on the Cob (see page 135)

Stuffed Tomatoes (see page 50)

Combine all the ingredients in a bowl and toss to mix and coat well. Cover and chill in the fridge for at least an hour, ideally 4 hours.

Preheat the air fryer to 180°C (350°F).

Place the chicken thighs in a single layer in the air fryer and pour any leftover marinade over them. Cook for 20–22 minutes, turning once, or until cooked through (if you have a meat thermometer, the internal temperature should be 74°C/165°F).

Serve with corn on the cob and stuffed tomatoes.

FISH TACOS
WITH MANGO & AVOCADO SALSA

There seems to be a host of processed ingredients in taco spice mixes. Simply raiding your spice cupboard will suffice when it comes to creating a delicious homemade version to make tasty, succulent fish tacos. The fresh salsa alongside is the perfect match.

½ teaspoon paprika

½ teaspoon ground cumin

good pinch of cayenne pepper

pinch of chilli flakes

½ teaspoon dried oregano

½ teaspoon garlic powder

½ teaspoon salt

1½ tablespoons extra virgin olive oil

500g (1lb 2oz) skinless white fish fillets

FOR THE MANGO & AVOCADO SALSA

1 ripe mango, finely diced

1 ripe avocado, finely diced

½ red onion, finely diced

½ red chilli, finely chopped

1 tablespoon white wine vinegar

1 tablespoon extra virgin olive oil

1 tablespoon lime juice

2 tablespoons chopped fresh coriander

TO SERVE

16 mini or 8 standard UPF-free tortillas

soured cream (optional)

Preheat the air fryer to 190°C (375°F).

Mix the spices, oregano, garlic powder and salt in a bowl, then place on a plate.

Brush the olive oil over both sides of the fish fillets, then press the top side of each fillet into the spice mix.

Place the fillets, spice side up, on a piece of greaseproof paper, then carefully place in the air fryer and cook for 8–10 minutes, or until cooked through (if you have a meat thermometer, the internal temperature should be 63°C/145°F). Remove from the air fryer and use a fork to flake the fish.

Meanwhile, make the salsa by mixing all the ingredients in a bowl.

Serve the spiced fish on the tortillas with the fresh salsa, along with soured cream, if you like.

SIDES

BABY CARROTS WITH GINGER & HONEY

One of the many reasons we are so drawn to processed foods is that the food industry has done a great job of understanding our love for a sweet and savoury combination. This recipe marries sweet and savoury perfectly without a processed ingredient in sight. Not only that, there are few more delicious combinations than carrots, ginger and honey.

SERVES 2

200g (7oz) baby carrots, scrubbed

30g (1oz) unsalted butter

¼ teaspoon salt

⅛ teaspoon pepper

¼ teaspoon ground ginger

¼ teaspoon ground cinnamon

1 tablespoon runny honey

chopped parsley, to serve

Preheat the air fryer to 180°C (350°F).

Arrange the carrots in a single layer in a heatproof dish that fits in the air fryer – if you have a smaller air fryer, you may need to cook in batches.

Place the butter on top, scatter over the salt, pepper, ginger and cinnamon, then drizzle over the honey. Wrap the dish in foil and cook in the air fryer for 10 minutes.

Remove the foil and cook for a further 15 minutes, or until the carrots just give when pierced with a fork. Scatter with chopped parsley to serve.

CORN ON THE COB

Cooking corn on the cob in the air fryer brings out the sweetness of every kernel. Simply serve with a little melted butter.

4 corn cobs, husks and silk removed

2 tablespoons extra virgin olive oil

salt

butter, to serve

Preheat the air fryer to 190°C (375°F).

Break the corn cobs in half by using a sharp knife to make an indentation, then snapping them with your hands. Rub the olive oil, then a little salt on to the pieces, and cook in the air fryer, turning once, for 8 minutes or until tender. Serve hot with butter.

SLOW-ROASTED GARLICKY TOMATOES

When you think of an air fryer as a small oven, slow-roasting foods in a faster time than in a normal oven becomes a distinct possibility. These tomatoes certainly benefit from a lower and slower method of cooking.

SERVES 4

6 plum tomatoes, halved lengthways

2 teaspoons extra virgin olive oil

4 plump garlic cloves

3 tablespoons torn basil leaves

salt and pepper

Preheat the air fryer to 100°C (210°F).

Toss the tomato halves with half the olive oil and some salt and pepper. Cook in the air fryer with the unpeeled garlic cloves alongside for 1½ hours.

Squeeze the garlic from its skin over the tomatoes, scatter with the basil, drizzle with the remaining olive oil and season again with a little more salt and pepper, if desired.

ROASTED NEW POTATOES

A classic flavour combination – potatoes with garlic and rosemary. The paprika adds a natural smokiness. Choose potatoes about 3–4cm (1¼–1½ inches) in length.

300g (10½oz) baby new potatoes, quartered

1 tablespoon extra virgin olive oil

¼ teaspoon garlic powder

¼ teaspoon dried rosemary

½ teaspoon salt

¼ teaspoon smoked paprika

¼ teaspoon pepper

Preheat the air fryer to 200°C (400°F).

Toss the potatoes with all the remaining ingredients in a heatproof dish that fits in the air fryer. Cook in the air fryer for 15–18 minutes, or until the potatoes are crispy on the outside but soft on the inside when pierced with a fork.

MISO-GLAZED AUBERGINES

Miso paste is a great store cupboard staple for adding umami (our fifth taste, described as a 'rich savouriness'). Combining the sweetness of honey and saltiness of soy sauce, this miso glaze makes for tender and moist aubergines that work wonderfully well as a vegetable side dish. They go well with the Pork & Hoisin Meatballs on page 64, or the Japanese-Style 'Fried' Chicken on page 116.

SERVES 4

- 2 aubergines, stems removed, halved lengthways
- 2 tablespoons extra virgin olive oil
- 2 teaspoons white miso paste
- 1 tablespoon runny honey
- 1 tablespoon soy sauce
- juice of ½ lime
- 2 spring onions, finely chopped
- salt

Preheat the air fryer to 180°C (350°F).

Use a sharp knife to score a criss-cross pattern on the cut surfaces of the aubergine halves – the cuts should be about 1.5cm (⅝ inch) apart and 5mm (¼ inch) deep.

Brush the aubergines with half the olive oil and sprinkle with salt. Cook in the air fryer for 10 minutes with the cut sides up, then turn them and cook for a further 5 minutes. If you have a smaller air fryer, you may need to do this in batches.

Prepare the miso glaze by combining the miso paste, honey, soy sauce and remaining olive oil in a small bowl.

Turn the aubergines cut sides up once again, then pour the miso glaze evenly over each half, spreading with the back of a spoon. Cook for a further 5 minutes, or until tender. Serve sprinkled with the lime juice and spring onions.

RATATOUILLE

This simple Provençal dish is so easy to make. Cans of ratatouille are extremely convenient but are more expensive and contain added starches. It seems a no-brainer to batch-cook ratatouille for several meals at a time. If you don't have herbes de Provence, use ½ teaspoon of dried oregano, ¼ teaspoon of dried thyme and ¼ teaspoon of dried basil instead. I like to serve this with the Squash, Sausage & Crispy Kale Bake (see page 60).

SERVES 4

1 aubergine, cut into rough 2cm (¾ inch) cubes

1 red pepper, cored, deseeded and diced

12 cherry tomatoes

1 small courgette, cut into rough 2cm (¾ inch) cubes

3 tablespoons extra virgin olive oil

1 teaspoon herbes de Provence

½ teaspoon salt

¼ teaspoon pepper

Preheat the air fryer to 180°C (350°F).

In a large bowl, toss all the ingredients together to coat well.

Cook the vegetables in the air fryer, turning a couple of times during cooking, for 20–25 minutes, or until the aubergine is soft and cooked through. Serve with your favourite dish.

MEDITERRANEAN VEG & COUSCOUS SALAD

This makes a delicious salad that works with so many of the main dishes in this book, especially the Halloumi & Courgette Kebabs on page 54. Increasingly, we are in a grab-and-go culture when it comes to quick-and-easy lunches. Salads like this are available at many outlets, yet they often contain stabilizers and preservatives, unlike this homemade version. This recipe makes enough for 8 portions – if you have a smaller air fryer, simply halve it.

SERVES 8

2 red peppers, cored, deseeded and diced

1 red onion, cut into 8 wedges

1 courgette, cut into 2cm (¾ inch) cubes

1 aubergine, cut into 2cm (¾ inch) cubes

2 tablespoons extra virgin olive oil

¾ teaspoon salt

½ teaspoon ground cinnamon

1 teaspoon ground cumin

1 teaspoon ground coriander

½ teaspoon garlic powder

200g (7oz) couscous

chopped parsley, to serve

FOR THE DRESSING

4 tablespoons extra virgin olive oil

½ teaspoon cayenne pepper

1 tablespoon ground cumin

1 tablespoon tomato purée

2 tablespoons lime juice

¼ teaspoon salt

¼ teaspoon pepper

Preheat the air fryer to 180°C (350°F).

Toss all the vegetables with the olive oil and all the spices in a large mixing bowl to coat. Pour into a heatproof dish that fits in the air fryer and cook for 20–25 minutes, or until soft and ever so slightly charred at the edges.

Meanwhile, mix all the dressing ingredients in a small bowl. Soak the couscous according to the packet instructions, then allow to cool a little before mixing in the cooked vegetables and the dressing and stirring well. Serve scattered with chopped parsley.

MAPLE-ROASTED ROOT VEGETABLES

A wonderful sweet and savoury combination, this recipe provides a good healthy dose of beta-carotene.

SERVES 4

1 large sweet potato, peeled and cut into 2cm (¾ inch) cubes

2 carrots, cut into 1cm (½ inch) cubes

½ butternut squash, flesh cut into 1.5cm (⅝ inch) cubes

1 tablespoon extra virgin olive oil

½ teaspoon salt

¼ teaspoon pepper

1 tablespoon maple syrup

Preheat the air fryer to 180°C (350°F).

Toss the vegetables with all the remaining ingredients in a bowl to coat. Cook in the air fryer for 20 minutes, tossing once during cooking, or until the vegetables are cooked through.

SPICY PATATAS BRAVAS

A traditional Spanish favourite. These crispy air-fried potatoes are served with a spicy and smoky sauce.

300g (10½oz) potatoes, cut into 1.5cm (⅝ inch) cubes

2 teaspoons extra virgin olive oil

salt

FOR THE SAUCE

2 shallots, finely chopped

½ red chilli, finely chopped

1 plump garlic clove, finely chopped

2 tablespoons extra virgin olive oil

¼ teaspoon Vegetable Stock Paste (see page 10)

¼ teaspoon unrefined sugar

200g (7oz) canned tomatoes

Cook the chopped potatoes in a saucepan of salted boiling water for 5 minutes, until they just give when pierced with a fork. Drain, then leave to air dry.

Preheat the air fryer to 190°C (375°F).

Toss the potatoes with the olive oil and ¼ teaspoon of salt, then cook in the air fryer for 20 minutes, or until crispy on the outside but soft inside.

Meanwhile, for the sauce, sauté the shallots, chilli and garlic in the olive oil in a small pan over a medium heat for about 5 minutes, until the shallots are soft. Add the stock paste, sugar and canned tomatoes. Reduce the heat a little and simmer for 10 minutes. Remove from the heat and pour over the cooked potatoes in a serving bowl.

TANDOORI CAULIFLOWER

A tasty, healthy and flavourful side dish. Tender cauliflower florets are coated with savoury, slightly smoky and earthy spices, then roasted until crisp.

400g (14oz) small cauliflower florets

2 tablespoons extra virgin olive oil

1 teaspoon ground coriander

1 teaspoon paprika

½ teaspoon ground cumin

½ teaspoon ground turmeric

½ teaspoon garam masala

½ teaspoon salt

1 tablespoon chopped garlic

1 tablespoon (peeled) chopped fresh root ginger

Toss all the ingredients together in a large bowl until well coated. Leave covered at room temperature for 30 minutes.

Preheat the air fryer to 180°C (350°F).

Cook the cauliflower in a single layer in the air fryer for 20–25 minutes, or until it just gives when pierced with a fork.

RAS-EL-HANOUT & HONEY-ROASTED VEGETABLES

Ras-el-hanout is possibly one of the tastiest spice mixes you'll find. It lends itself so well to a honey and vegetable pairing. This side goes exceptionally well with the Lamb Kofta Burgers on page 57.

Lamb Kofta Burgers on page 57.

SERVES 2

150g (5½oz) cauliflower

1 teaspoon runny honey

1 teaspoon ras-el-hanout

1 tablespoon extra virgin olive oil

¼ teaspoon salt

200g (7oz) butternut squash flesh, cut into 2cm (¾ inch) cubes

Preheat the air fryer to 180°C (350°F).

Divide the cauliflower into small florets and cut the stems into 1cm (½ inch) cubes.

Combine the honey, ras-el-hanout, oil and salt in a heatproof dish that fits in the air fryer, then toss the vegetables in this mixture. Cook in the air fryer, stirring the vegetables a couple of times, for 20 minutes or until they are soft and cooked through.

ROASTED ALOO GOBI

This wonderful Indian side dish is made up of cauliflower, potatoes and tomatoes, air-fried in oil and spices. The squeeze of lime juice at the end of cooking elevates the taste of this dish even further. You don't need to peel the potato for this one.

SERVES 4

400g (14oz) cauliflower florets

1 potato, about 200g (7oz), cut into 1cm (½ inch) cubes

1 onion, thickly sliced

150g (5½oz) tomatoes, cut into 2cm (¾ inch) cubes

2 tablespoons extra virgin olive oil or avocado oil

½ teaspoon garlic powder

½ teaspoon ground cumin

½ teaspoon ground turmeric

1 teaspoon ground coriander

½ teaspoon chilli powder

1 teaspoon salt

1 teaspoon lime juice

1 tablespoon chopped fresh coriander

Preheat the air fryer to 190°C (375°F).

Toss the cauliflower, potato, onion and tomatoes with the oil, spices and salt to coat. Cook in a single layer in the air fryer for 25–30 minutes, tossing once or twice during cooking, or until the potato cubes are soft when pierced with a fork. If you have a smaller air fryer, you may need to do this in batches. Serve drizzled with the lime juice and scattered with the coriander.

SNACKS

APPLE CHIPS

A lovely snack. Cooking apple chips in an air fryer is a great way of intensifying the apple flavour and making them even sweeter in the process.

SERVES 1–2

1 apple, cored but skin left on

Preheat the air fryer to 190°C (375°F).

Using a mandolin or the slicing side of a box grater, very thinly slice the apple into extremely thin rings.

Lay out the apple rings in the air fryer and cover with a grill rack to stop them flying around during cooking. Cook for 8 minutes, turning them half way through cooking, or until they have curled up at the edges and browned slightly.

Remove from the air fryer and leave to crisp up further. Serve on the day of cooking.

GRANOLA

As many shop-bought granolas contain added flavourings and sweeteners, making your own means you're in control. Ginger and cinnamon add warming spice and maple syrup makes this granola feel luxurious. Make sure you line the air fryer with nonstick baking paper just before adding the granola – don't line the air fryer while preheating or the paper will be drawn into the fan and may catch fire. Serve the granola for breakfast or brunch with Greek yogurt.

SERVES 4

60g (2¼oz) coconut oil, melted

50g (1¾oz) maple syrup

½ teaspoon ground ginger

¾ teaspoon ground cinnamon

20g (¾oz) pumpkin seeds

15g (½oz) chia seeds

100g (3½oz) rolled oats

20g (¾oz) flaked almonds

10g (¼oz) desiccated coconut

Preheat the air fryer to 160°C (325°F).

Mix the coconut oil with the maple syrup, ginger and cinnamon in a small bowl.

In a larger bowl, combine the pumpkin seeds, chia seeds and oats. Stir the coconut oil mix into the dry ingredients.

Line the base of the air fryer with nonstick baking paper, then spread out the granola in an even layer on top. Cook for 15 minutes, stirring twice during cooking.

Remove from the air fryer, then stir in the almonds and coconut. Leave to cool, then store in an airtight container for up to 3 days.

CANDIED WALNUTS

These crunchy caramelized nuts are a great party snack. You can also serve them as a salad topper, or sprinkled over Greek yogurt.

3 tablespoons honey

2 tablespoons water

½ teaspoon vanilla extract

½ teaspoon ground cinnamon

½ teaspoon salt

200g (7oz) walnuts

Preheat the air fryer to 180°C (350°F).

Mix the honey, water, vanilla, cinnamon and salt in a bowl, toss in the walnuts and stir to coat well.

Spread out the walnuts in a single layer in a baking tin that fits in the air fryer, then cook for 8 minutes, stirring a couple of times as the nuts cook. Stir once more, then leave to cool completely.

Store in an airtight container for up to 3 days.

MOROCCAN-STYLE CARROT HUMMUS

SERVES 8

Most shop-bought hummus contains preservatives and often other ultra-processed ingredients too. This recipe combines the sweet earthiness of carrots with classic North African spices.

400g (14oz) carrots, peeled and cut into 2cm (¾ inch) batons

2 tablespoons olive oil

1 large garlic clove, peeled

2 tablespoons tahini

120g (4¼oz) drained canned chickpeas

juice of 1 lemon

salt and pepper

FOR THE SPICE MIX

2 teaspoons extra virgin olive oil

½ teaspoon ground cumin

½ teaspoon ground ginger

½ teaspoon salt

¼ teaspoon cayenne pepper

¼ teaspoon ground allspice

¼ teaspoon ground coriander

¼ teaspoon unrefined sugar

Preheat the air fryer to 180°C (350°F).

Toss the carrots with the spice mix ingredients in a bowl until well coated. Cook in a single layer in the air fryer for 20 minutes, or until they just give when pierced with a fork. Allow to cool a little.

Place the carrots in a food processor with all the remaining ingredients and blitz until smooth, adding a little water to loosen the mixture to your desired texture.

ROASTED PEPPER & WALNUT DIP

SERVES 3–4

Even fresh shop-bought dips tend to have added starches or stabilizers. Making your own, especially when they're as quick and easy as this one, just makes sense.

3 Romano peppers

2 tablespoons extra virgin olive oil, plus extra for brushing

50g (1¾oz) walnuts

50g (1¾oz) fresh breadcrumbs from a rustic loaf

1 teaspoon ground cumin

2 teaspoons runny honey

juice of ½ small lemon

¼ teaspoon salt

handful of pomegranate seeds, to serve

Preheat the air fryer to 180°C (350°F).

Brush the peppers with a little olive oil, then cook in the air fryer for 10 minutes, or until soft. Place the walnuts in a heatproof dish that fits in the air fryer and toast for 2 minutes.

Remove the stems and seeds from the peppers when cool enough to handle. Grind the toasted walnuts in a food processor to a consistency as close to ground almonds as possible, then add all the other ingredients and blitz until smooth. Serve scattered with pomegranate seeds.

AUBERGINE & YOGURT DIP

Serve this lovely dip with the Garlic Pitta Chips on page 163, or as a side with the Lamb Kofta Burgers on page 57.

2 aubergines, halved lengthways

½ teaspoon salt

1 tablespoon extra virgin olive oil

2 large garlic cloves

juice of 1 lemon

1 teaspoon ground cumin

200g (7oz) Greek yogurt

1 teaspoon finely chopped mint leaves

salt and pepper

Preheat the air fryer to 180°C (350°F).

Gently score the cut sides of the aubergine halves in a criss-cross pattern and rub in the salt and olive oil to completely cover the cut surfaces. Cook in the air fryer, in batches if necessary, with the whole unpeeled garlic cloves for 20–25 minutes, or until very soft. The surfaces will become very dark; this adds to the flavour. Remove from the air fryer and set aside for a few minutes until cool enough to handle.

Scoop out the aubergine flesh and place in a food processor. Squeeze in the garlic flesh, discarding the skin, and add the lemon juice, cumin, yogurt and mint, then blitz until smooth. Season to taste before serving.

UPF-FREE TORTILLA CHIPS

These crispy chips are ideal for scooping up mouthfuls of the dips in this book. Choose tortilla wraps with as few ingredients as possible, ideally just flour, water, oil and salt.

2 UPF-free wholegrain tortilla wraps, cut into wedges

1 tablespoon extra virgin olive oil

½ teaspoon fine salt

Preheat the air fryer to 200°C (400°F).

Brush the tortilla wedges with the olive oil and sprinkle with the salt. Cook in in a single layer the air fryer for 2 minutes on each side, turning carefully half way through cooking.

PADRÓN PEPPERS

SERVES 2

Salty, blistered peppers, perfect for a healthy snack.

250g (9oz) padrón peppers

2 teaspoons extra virgin olive oil

sea salt flakes, to serve

Preheat the air fryer to 200°C (400°F).

Toss the peppers in the olive oil. Place in the air fryer in a single layer, then cook for 5 minutes, or until the skins start to blister. Remove from the air fryer, sprinkle over flaky sea salt, then serve hot.

GARLIC PITTA CHIPS

SERVES 2

Pitta breads are among the least processed bread products available in supermarkets. While humble pittas seem to have been overtaken by wraps in terms of popularity, they contain far fewer ingredients. This recipe makes use of the high heat and fast cooking speed of an air fryer to create crisp pitta chips in minutes. They are the perfect accompaniment to the Aubergine & Yogurt Dip on page 160.

20g (¾oz) Garlic Butter (see page 11)

2 pitta breads

Preheat the air fryer to 180°C (350°F).

Spread the garlic butter evenly over one side of each pitta, then cut the pittas into 12 pieces each.

Place the pittas in the air fryer in a single layer without overlapping, butter sides up, and cook for 4 minutes, then turn and cook for a further 2 minutes. Cook in 2 batches if you have a smaller air fryer.

CHILLI & LIME CHICKPEAS

These are a delightful and versatile snack. They can also be used as a salad topper to give some texture, rather like croûtons.

400g (14oz) can chickpeas, drained, rinsed and patted dry

½ teaspoon chilli powder

½ teaspoon ground cumin

½ teaspoon smoked paprika

½ teaspoon salt

1 tablespoon extra virgin olive oil

grated zest of 1 lime, plus wedges to serve

Preheat the air fryer to 180°C (350°F).

Toss the chickpeas in a bowl with the spices and salt to coat, then add the olive oil, toss again, then add the lime zest and stir well.

Cook in a single layer in the air fryer for 12 minutes, stirring the chickpeas twice during cooking.

Allow to cool before serving with lime wedges, if you like.

PARMA HAM CHIPS

These super-tasty and crispy chips are made from just one ingredient, made crispy in the air fryer. Why Parma ham? Because it is usually made to a traditional standard without any preservatives. These make an ideal snack to offer friends with a drink.

SERVES 4

8 slices of Parma ham

Preheat the air fryer to 180°C (350°F).

Cook the Parma ham in a single layer in the air fryer for 4 minutes, cooking in batches if necessary. Remove and allow to cool on kitchen paper to absorb the excess fat. When fully cool, break the crispy ham into shards before serving.

SPICED CASHEWS

A great spicy snack and an ideal alternative to crisps or some of the commercially available coated nuts sold in stores.

200g (7oz) cashews (unsalted and unroasted)

2 teaspoons extra virgin olive oil

½ teaspoon smoked paprika

½ teaspoon ground cumin

½ teaspoon ground coriander

½ teaspoon coconut sugar

pinch of salt

Preheat the air fryer to 150°C (300°F).

Combine all the ingredients in a bowl and toss well to coat. Spread out in a single layer on a piece of greaseproof paper in the air fryer and cook for 12 minutes, stirring twice during cooking. Allow to cool before serving.

CASHEW BUTTER

This is very similar to peanut butter in texture but has a slightly sweeter taste. It's great on toast or stirred into porridge and the good news is you can make it with just two ingredients.

300g (10½oz) cashews (unsalted and unroasted)

¼ teaspoon salt

Preheat the air fryer to 180°C (350°F).

Place the nuts on a piece of greaseproof paper or in a heatproof dish that fits in the air fryer, preferably in a single layer. Cook in the air fryer for 3–4 minutes, or until they're turning a little golden in colour.

Place the nuts and salt in a high-speed blender and blend for up to 10 minutes, or until smooth, scraping down the sides several times. If your blender is not a high-speed model, you may need to add a little flavourless oil such as avocado oil to bind it. Store in a clean jar in the fridge for up to 2 weeks.

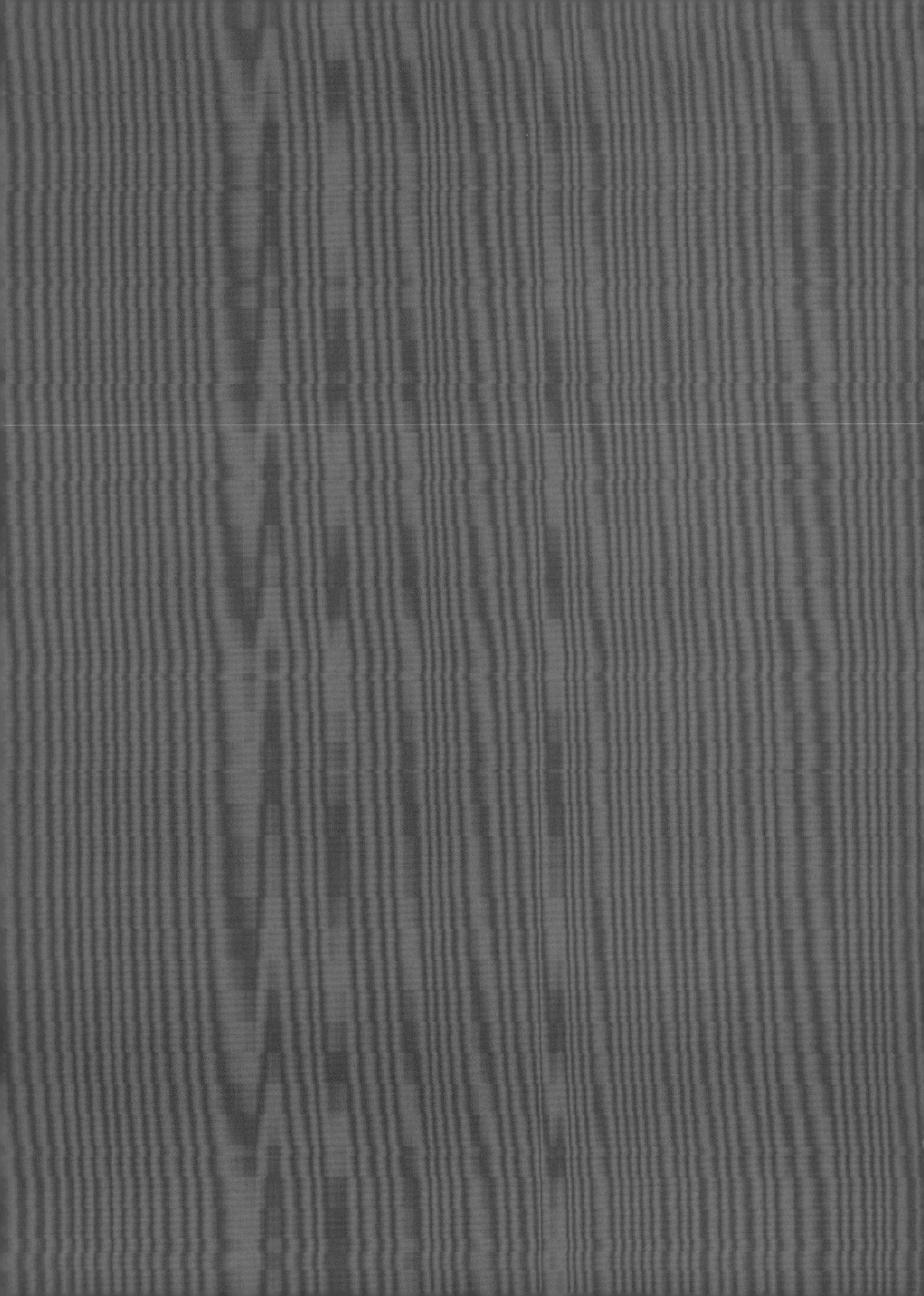

DESSERTS

BAKED STRAWBERRY 'CHEESECAKES'

Although these don't contain any cheese, they are similar in taste and texture to those little pots of cheesecake you can buy in the supermarket. Those pots often contain sweeteners, modified starches, colours, preservatives and flavourings, but these pots, made in your air fryer, use just yogurt, cream, condensed milk and strawberries to create a delicious dessert.

SERVES 2–3

100ml (3½fl oz) condensed milk

100ml (3½fl oz) double cream

100g (3½oz) Greek yogurt

4 strawberries, finely chopped

Preheat the air fryer to 150°C (300°F).

Stir the condensed milk, cream and yogurt together in a jug, then divide between 2–3 deep ramekins (the number you can fill may depend on the size of your ramekins). Place the ramekins in a heatproof dish that fits in the air fryer and pour cold water into the dish to about three-quarters full.

Carefully place the dish in the air fryer and cook for 15 minutes, or until the mixture is slightly browned and almost set. Cool, then chill in the fridge until ready to serve. Top with the strawberries just before serving.

BAKED CHOCOLATE BANANAS

There's something reminiscent of childhood camping trips about these bananas.

2 whole bananas

20g (¾oz) dark chocolate chips or chunks

TO SERVE (OPTIONAL)
Greek yogurt
chopped walnuts

Preheat the air fryer to 180°C (350°F).

Make a deep cut lengthways along each banana, following the curve. Open slightly and push the chocolate into the cuts.

Wrap the bananas in nonstick baking paper or foil to fully enclose them. Cook in the air fryer for 20 minutes, or until soft and jammy inside, checking by opening the foil slightly.

Serve hot with Greek yogurt and chopped walnuts, if you like.

BANANA FLAPJACKS

Flapjacks make a delicious wholegrain dessert. Many shop-bought versions contain a lot of sugar and often margarine. This recipe uses bananas to reduce the refined sugar content and butter to avoid overly-processed ingredients.

30g (1oz) butter, melted, plus extra for buttering the tin

160g (5¾oz) ripe banana (peeled weight), mashed

20g (¾oz) runny honey

½ teaspoon ground cinnamon

110g (3¾oz) rolled oats

Preheat the air fryer to 170°C (340°F).

Butter and line a 15cm (6 inch) square baking tin or an equivalent size that fits in your air fryer.

Mix all the ingredients together in a bowl, then press the mixture into the prepared tin in an even layer. Cook in the air fryer for 20 minutes. Remove, allow to cool, then slice into 6 portions to serve.

BAKED CINNAMON NECTARINES

Possibly one of the best summer desserts. A delightful and simple dessert that highlights the natural sweetness of the fruit. The nectarines are enhanced with a drizzle of maple syrup and a sprinkle of cinnamon to create a warm and aromatic treat.

SERVES 4

4 nectarines, ripe but still firm

2 teaspoons maple syrup

1 teaspoon ground cinnamon

Greek yogurt, to serve

Preheat the air fryer to 180°C (350°F).

Cut the nectarines in half and remove the stones. Place the halves, cut sides up, in a heatproof dish that fits in the air fryer.

Mix together the maple syrup and cinnamon and drizzle over the nectarine halves. Cook in the air fryer for 15–20 minutes, until soft and jammy. These are best served hot with Greek yogurt.

BANANA & CHIA MUFFINS

While a whole tray of muffins is great for a bake sale or gathering, there are times when you'd simply like a little sweet treat. Shop-bought muffins often contain sweeteners, flavourings, starches, preservatives and emulsifiers. These banana muffins are so simple and quick to make.

MAKES 6

2 ripe bananas, about 200g (7oz) peeled weight, mashed

2 teaspoons chia seeds mixed with 2 tablespoons lukewarm water

50g (2oz) coconut oil, melted

a few drops of vanilla extract

40g (1½oz) unrefined sugar

125g (4½oz) self-raising flour

Preheat the air fryer to 150°C (300°F).

Place the bananas, chia and water mix, coconut oil and vanilla extract in a bowl, then stir in the sugar and flour. Divide the mixture evenly between 6 paper or silicone cupcake cases.

Cook in the air fryer for 13–15 minutes, or until a cocktail stick inserted into the middle of a muffin comes out clean. Allow to cool before serving. These are best eaten on the day they are made.

BERRY CHIA COMPOTE WITH GREEK YOGURT

Chia seeds, when combined with liquid, naturally become thick and gloopy. This quality makes them perfect for thickening roasted berries and their juices, creating a low-sugar, high-fibre alternative to jam.

300g (10½oz) frozen blueberries or blackberries

juice of ½ lemon

about 1 tablespoon maple syrup, to taste

3 tablespoons chia seeds

Greek yogurt, to serve

Preheat the air fryer to 170°C (340°F).

Place the frozen berries, lemon juice and maple syrup in a heatproof dish that fits in the air fryer and stir together. Cook in the air fryer for 10–12 minutes until the berries have started to collapse, then remove from the air fryer.

Crush the berries with a fork. Stir in the chia seeds, then leave the mixture to cool and thicken. Serve with Greek yogurt.

COURGETTE BROWNIES

This egg-free recipe makes the most of the moisture naturally present in courgettes to create these delicious brownies.

MAKES 9

80g (2¾oz) avocado oil or other flavourless oil, plus extra for greasing the tin

200g (7oz) courgettes, finely grated

2 teaspoons vanilla extract

135g (4¾oz) unrefined sugar

150g (5½oz) plain flour

35g (1¼oz) cacao powder

1 teaspoon bicarbonate of soda

½ teaspoon salt

50g (1¾oz) dark chocolate chips

Combine the avocado oil, grated courgette and vanilla extract in one bowl and the dry ingredients in another, then stir them together. Add the chocolate chips and stir to combine. Leave to settle for 20–30 minutes to allow the courgette to release its moisture.

Preheat the air fryer to 160°C (325°F). Grease and line a 15cm (6 inch) square baking tin or an equivalent size that fits in your air fryer.

Transfer the mixture to the prepared tin and press into an even layer with the back of a spoon. Cook in the air fryer for 35–40 minutes, or until a cocktail stick inserted into the middle comes out clean. If you prefer a slightly softer brownie, then a little wet mixture on the cocktail stick is fine. Allow to cool, then slice into 9 portions to serve.

FRUIT CRUMBLE POTS

Shop-bought fruit crumble often contains added sweeteners, starches and emulsifiers. These little crumble pots use only ingredients you'll find in your home kitchen. The use of frozen raspberries makes this an all-year-round dessert.

SERVES 2

125g (4½oz) frozen raspberries

15g (½oz or 1 tablespooon) runny honey

25g (1oz) rolled oats

25g (1oz) plain flour

5g (⅛oz or 1 teaspoon) unrefined sugar (I use coconut sugar)

25g (1oz) salted butter, melted

Greek yogurt, to serve

Preheat the air fryer to 180°C (350°F).

Mix the frozen raspberries and honey in a bowl and leave to defrost a little while you prepare the crumble topping.

Combine the oats, flour, sugar and melted butter in a bowl to make a crumble mixture.

Equally divide the raspberries between 2 deep ramekins. Top with the crumble and cook in the air fryer for 13–15 minutes, or until the crumble is golden brown on top. Cool a little, then serve with a good dollop of Greek yogurt.

INDIVIDUAL BREAD & BUTTER PUDDINGS

Not only will you have heard of the ingredients in this homemade bread and butter pudding recipe (unlike those found in commercial products), this uses up leftover bread, and you can decide on the level of sweetness, depending on your personal preference.

SERVES 2

- 15g (½oz) salted butter
- 2 slices of sourdough bread, crusts removed
- 20g (¾oz) raisins
- 30g (1oz) unsulphured dried apricots, chopped
- 1 egg
- 25ml (¾fl oz) double cream
- 80ml (2¾fl oz) milk
- 2 teaspoons maple syrup
- ½ teaspoon ground cinnamon
- ¼ teaspoon ground ginger
- natural yogurt or cream, to serve

Preheat the air fryer to 180°C (350°F).

Spread the butter over both sides of each slice of bread, then tear into pieces. Divide half the pieces of bread between 2 deep ramekins. Scatter over half the dried fruit, then top with the remaining bread and scatter over the remaining dried fruit.

In a bowl, beat the egg, then whisk in the cream, milk, maple syrup and spices. Pour this evenly into the ramekins and press on the tops to ensure the dried fruit is covered by the liquid.

Cook in the air fryer for 12 minutes, or until the tops are golden and the insides just set. Allow to cool until you can handle the ramekins, then enjoy just warm with yogurt or cream.

SIMPLE BANANA BREAD

Why heat your whole oven to bake one loaf of banana bread, when you can heat just your air fryer? This six-ingredient banana bread couldn't be simpler. It's easy to prepare and cooks quickly too.

SERVES 8

4 very ripe bananas

1 large egg, beaten

75g (2¾oz) butter, softened, plus extra to serve (optional)

1 teaspoon vanilla extract

65g (2¼oz) unrefined sugar, such as coconut sugar

170g (6oz) self-raising flour

oil, to grease the tin

Preheat the air fryer to 150°C (300°F). Grease and line a 450g (1lb) loaf tin.

Blitz the peeled bananas, egg, butter and vanilla in a food processor or blender until smooth. Add the sugar and flour and blend until just mixed.

Pour into prepared tin and cook in the air fryer for 45 minutes, or until a cocktail stick inserted into the middle comes out clean. Leave to cool for a few minutes, then remove from the tin. Serve this in slices, with butter if you like.

CHOCOLATE OAT COOKIES

There are so many 'high fibre' grab-and-go products in the shops, yet when you look at the ingredients, the high fibre benefits seem to get lost in a sea of added ingredients you simply wouldn't find in your home store cupboard. These cookies are certainly high in fibre and yet you'll recognize all the ingredients too.

MAKES 3

55g (2oz) rolled oats

1 tablespoon cacao powder

½ teaspoon baking powder

2 tablespoons chia seeds

3 tablespoons dark chocolate chips or chunks

1 tablespoon maple syrup

1 ripe banana, mashed

1 teaspoon water

Combine all the ingredients in a mixing bowl and stir well. Leave to settle for 30 minutes to allow the cookie dough to thicken.

Preheat the air fryer to 160°C (325°F).

Shape the dough into 3 cookies and place on a piece of greaseproof paper. Cook in the air fryer, ensuring they are in a single layer and not overlapping, for 15 minutes, then allow to cool just a little and enjoy just warm.

RAPPLEJACKS

These really moist, apple and oat slices have a jammy raspberry topping. If you don't have a 20cm (8 inch) square baking tin, or it won't fit in your air fryer, use a 15cm (6 inch) square tin instead and cook the rapplejacks for a bit longer as the flapjack will have a thicker base.

225g (8oz) frozen raspberries

3 tablespoons runny honey

130g (4¾oz) butter

2 apples, grated with their skin on

180g (6¼oz) rolled oats

1 teaspoon ground ginger

1 teaspoon ground cinnamon

Place the frozen raspberries in a bowl and drizzle over 1 tablespoon of the honey. Set aside for 1 hour, then mash with a fork until it becomes a jammy consistency.

Preheat the air fryer to 170°C (340°F). Grease and line a 20cm (8 inch) square baking tin or an equivalent size that fits in your air fryer

Melt the butter and remaining honey in a saucepan, then add the grated apple, the oats, ginger and cinnamon, and stir well.

Press the mixture in an even layer in the prepared tin. Spread the mashed raspberries on top, then cook in the air fryer for 22–25 minutes, or until the top is starting to caramelize but not burn.

Allow to cool fully before slicing into 9 squares. Store in an airtight container at room temperature, or in the fridge if you like a slightly firmer texture.

INDEX

UK—US GLOSSARY

aubergine	eggplant	double cream	heavy cream
baking paper	parchment paper	gram flour	chickpea flour/besan
beetroot	beet	minced meat	ground meat
bicarbonate of soda	baking soda	plain flour	all-purpose flour
butter beans	lima beans	pumpkin seeds	pepitas
caster sugar	superfine sugar	peppers (red/orange)	bell peppers
chilli flakes	crushed red pepper	rocket	arugula
clingfilm	plastic wrap	rolled oats	oatmeal
coriander	cilantro	soured cream	sour cream
courgette	zucchini	spring onions	scallions
desiccated coconut	shredded coconut	sultanas	golden raisins

ACKNOWLEDGEMENTS

Writing this cookbook has been a journey filled with passion and immense learning. I couldn't have done it without the support of many wonderful people. To my family, thank you for your endless love and encouragement. Special thanks to my husband Werner, my son Sam and my daughter Amalie for tasting countless recipes and providing honest feedback.

A heartfelt thank you to my publisher Kate Fox at Octopus Publishing Group for her keen eye. Thank you to Clare, my photographer, whose stunning images bring these recipes to life. Thanks to my editorial and production team, including Sybella Stephens for her hard work and dedication.

I am immensely grateful to a very talented team of recipe testers including Jane Hills, Emma Cowling, June and Chris Bailey, Jen Roach, Phil Berry, Rachel Clarke as well as Marcus and Kathryn King.

To my agent, Jane Graham Maw, thank you for believing in this project and for your efforts in bringing this cookbook to life.

Lastly, to my readers – thank you for your support and for sharing in my love of scratch cooking. This book is for you, and I hope it brings joy and delicious moments to your kitchen.

With gratitude, Jenny Tschiesche